Northern and

Dialects of English

Northern and Insular Scots

Robert McColl Millar

Edinburgh University Press

© Robert McColl Millar, 2007

Edinburgh University Press Ltd
22 George Square, Edinburgh

Typeset in 10.5/12 Janson
by Servis Filmsetting Ltd, Manchester, and
printed and bound in Great Britain by
Cromwell Press, Trowbridge, Wilts

A CIP record for this book is available from the British Library

ISBN 978 0 7486 2316 7 (hardback)
ISBN 978 0 7486 2317 4 (paperback)

The right of Robert McColl Millar
to be identified as author of this work
has been asserted in accordance with
the Copyright, Designs and Patents Act 1988.

Contents

For recordings of the transcriptions in this book go to
www.lel.ed.ac.uk/dialects

Acknowledgements

In the first place, I want to thank everyone who spoke to us while we were carrying out fieldwork for this book; especially those who agreed to be recorded. In particular, I would like to thank those who were recorded in Orkney and Lossiemouth but whose conversations have not been transcribed due to a faulty Minidisc recorder. Although your speech is not represented here, the ideas and pointers you gave us have been invaluable.

Second, I am especially grateful to those who helped us set up interviews: John Burke, Peter Fraser, Madelaine and Rachel King, Ali Lumsden, Jack and Vanda Moodie, John Tallach and Nicola Thomson.

I also want to thank my colleagues here in Aberdeen: Barbara Fennell, Carmen Llamas, Derrick McClure and, in particular, Dom Watt, who has given me a great deal of help and encouragement with transcriptions. I would also like to mention two former colleagues, Thor-Sigurd Nilsen and Caroline Macafee, whose ideas and views helped shaped my approach to this book. My students, Barbara Loester and Sandra McRae, have taught me a great deal.

The research for this book would have been much more difficult without a grant for travel to Shetland from the British Association for Applied Linguistics.

Sarah Edwards has been a very patient and helpful editor. April McMahon's and Patrick Honeybone's comments on an earlier draft of this book were both generous and insightful. Many thanks also to Alison Sandison for her excellent maps.

Finally, my debt to Sandra Weyland is immense. Throughout the writing of this book, she has worked as (unpaid) research assistant while holding down a very demanding job. It is unlikely that I would have made half of the contacts across the Northern Isles and northern Scotland which she made. This book is dedicated to her.

1 Introduction

1.1 Northern and Insular Scots

This book is concerned with the Scots dialects of northern Scotland and the Northern Isles of Orkney and Shetland; dialects spoken by a wide variety of people living very different lives in divergent natural environments. Many speakers of the varieties concerned would be surprised to have their dialect included with some considered here, since many speakers see their dialects as being unique, even at a very local level. Yet all of these dialects are inter-related historically and culturally, even if particular dialects might be more closely connected to some members of the set than are others. They also share two further features. They are the most conservative dialects of Scots, being, at least until recently, vibrant features of the language use of almost all members of their communities. Dialect use has rarely been associated with a particular social class as is regularly the case elsewhere in the English-speaking world. Second, these dialects have all been affected by long-term contact with at least one other language.

These dialects, spoken in the North-East, the Black Isle, Caithness, Orkney and Shetland are relatives of, but not derived from, Standard English (although most inhabitants can also speak and write Scottish Standard English [SSE]). In their 'broadest' forms, these varieties are not intelligible to monodialectal speakers of any English variety spoken outside Scotland and Ulster. In the rest of northern Scotland, most inhabitants speak Highland English, essentially Standard English spoken with a Scottish accent, with some small-scale influence from Scots on lexis and structure, as well as phonological influence from Gaelic. Some still speak Gaelic as well.

Within the Scots-speaking regions, a number of different dialect areas are recognised by scholars. I have generally followed the classification of Johnson (1997) except when geographical terms are more transparent.

Map 1 Northern and Insular Scots

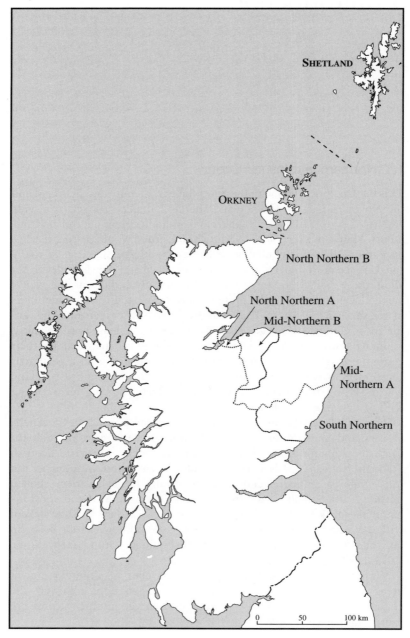

1.1.1 Northern Scots

As shown in the map above, the dialects of Northern Scots can be separated into three basic units: North Northern Scots, Mid-Northern Scots and a transitional area between Mid-Scots and Northern Scots termed South Northern. With the exception of South Northern Scots, all of these dialects are bounded on at least one side by the sea, and on another by areas where the local population spoke Gaelic until recently and where, in general, Highland English is now spoken. The boundary between Scots and Highland English is highly permeable.

1.1.1.1 Mid-Northern and South Northern Scots (North-East Scots)

Mid-Northern A is centred around the city of Aberdeen, although regional centres are also influential on their hinterlands. It comprises Aberdeenshire, as well as the part of Banffshire beside the sea and Kincardineshire (/kɪn'kardənʃɪr/) north of the Highland boundary fault, along with Stonehaven which, although in the Lowlands, is linguistically part of this unit. It is associated with the valleys of the rivers Dee, Ythan (/'aeθən/), Don and the northern part of the valley of the Deveron (/'divərɔn/).

Although, as we will see, differences exist between areas within this region, local dialects share many features. In brief, basing the boundaries on those of McClure (2002: 21–2; derived from Muirison [1963]), in traditional Mid-Northern A speakers pronounce the Scots equivalent to English *stone* as /stin/, although the equivalent to *home* is /hem/. The equivalent of English *moon* is pronounced /min/ and the sound spelled <wh> in English, pronounced as /ʍ/ or /hw/ in Mid-Scots, is traditionally pronounced /f/, whether as part of an interrogative pronoun, so that the equivalent to *what* is Mid-Northern A /fɪt/ or /fat/, or in any other context, so that the equivalent of *white* is /fəit/.

To the west of Mid-Northern A is Mid-Northern B, spoken in the upper part of Banffshire, all of the county of Moray and a small part of the north-east of Nairnshire. In this dialect the traditional equivalents to *moon*, and all of the <wh> words, no matter the word class, are the same as Mid-Northern A, but the equivalent of *stone* is pronounced with the same vowel as the equivalent of *home*: /sten/, /hem/. The rest of Nairnshire is a transitional zone both with North Northern A and Highland English. Many parts of this county were Gaelic-speaking well into the nineteenth century.

Most natives of the North-East call the local dialect *The Doric*; the local rural culture is also often termed *Doric*.

To the south of Mid-Northern A is South Northern Scots, spoken in the Mearns (Kincardineshire south of the Highland boundary fault) and northern and central Angus. South Northern is transitional between Northern and Mid-Scots. Following McClure's schematisation, traditional dialect speakers would, like Mid-Northern A speakers, pronounce the equivalent of *stone* as /stin/ and the equivalent to interrogative and relative pronouns such as *what* as /fɪt/, but the equivalent of *moon* in a number of ways which associate it with Mid-Scots or even Insular Scots (of which more in Chapter 2) rather than with Northern Scots of any type. Standard English <wh> words which are not interrogative or relative pronouns are pronounced with /ʍ/ or /hw/, not /f/, so that *white* would be /ʍəit/.

1.1.1.2 North Northern Scots

Unlike Mid-Northern, the North Northern dialects are not contiguous, instead representing former 'pockets' of Scots speech in a largely Gaelic-speaking area. To some extent all of these were previously settled by Gaelic or Scandinavian settlers, as well as demonstrating long term contact with the North-East and (in the case of Caithness) Orkney.

As shown in Map 3 (p. 9), North Northern A is associated primarily with Avoch (/ax/) and Cromarty on the Black Isle, with other small towns and villages on the Cromarty Firth, and to some extent with the east coast of Sutherland. Most of Nairnshire can be included in this area. A primary feature of the traditional dialects of the eastern Black Isle is that, unusually for Scots dialects, /h/ was not present in its historical contexts. Even more unusually, <wh> words were often pronounced without any initial consonant, so that the equivalent of *what* might be pronounced /ɪt/ or /at/.

North Northern B dialects are associated with Caithness, except for the mountainous south-west of the county. Caithness dialect has a variety of peculiarities which will be returned to on a number of occasions in this book. In a number of features it corresponds to Mid-Northern: for instance, <wh> words are pronounced /f/.

1.1.2 Insular Scots

It is much more straightforward to define boundaries between Insular Scots dialects than between North Northern, primarily because the speech communities are found in two discrete archipelagos. Within these archipelagos there is also considerable variation: between island and island and even within some of the larger islands. Nevertheless, all dialects share more with each other than they do with any other Scots dialects, perhaps primarily because of their recent Scandinavian connections. Both dialects use /no/ exclusively as their equivalent to Standard English *not.*

Insular A dialects are associated with the Orkney Isles. They share some features with north-eastern Caithness dialects. At least until recently, the second-person singular pronoun equivalent to archaic *thou* was /θu/. This form is highly recessive, if present at all, in mainland dialects.

Insular B dialects are associated with the Shetland Isles, including Fair Isle. Use of Scandinavian dialects only ceased in these islands in the eighteenth century. Scandinavian influence is pervasive in the local dialects. The second-person singular pronoun is /du/, which is used regularly by dialect speakers.

All of these points will be discussed in greater depth in later chapters of this book.

1.2 The linguistic ecologies of the regions

Essential to our understanding of these dialects is *marginality.* I am aware that *marginal* can be interpreted as meaning unimportant and far away. This is not my intention, however. The north of Scotland and the Northern Isles are only marginal in terms of the English-speaking world. The area is central to itself and open to influence from its neighbours down the east coast of Britain, in Scandinavia and the Baltic territories.

But the region *is* marginal in relation to the West Germanic languages. Northern Scotland was originally Gaelic-speaking. The Northern Scots dialects were formed during a period of long-term bilingualism between the incoming Anglian dialect and the native Celtic language. In some parts of northern Scotland, and in particular in the Northern Isles, a much closer relative of Scots was the primary contact language: the western varieties of Norse once spoken across the North Atlantic from Caithness, through Orkney, Shetland, the Faeroes and Iceland, to Greenland. In Caithness, Scots speakers came into contact with both Gaelic and Norse. Both of these languages have had significant effects upon the Scots spoken in the region.

The area is also marginal geographically. With the exception of its southern fringes, situated in the great valley of Strathmore and much more open to contact from the south, most of the Scots-speaking parts of mainland northern Scotland are, even today, not terribly accessible.

It was also marginal in the modern age in terms of its contact with an economy based upon industrial production. Industrialisation *did* happen in this area, most notably in Aberdeen. Nevertheless, elements of modern life in other parts of Scotland, such as the development of capitalist agriculture, were late to come to our area. Until the middle of the twentieth century, the majority of inhabitants of northern Scotland and the Northern Isles were involved in primary production of a traditional nature, such as farming and fishing. Particularly in the Northern Isles, many people lived at or near subsistence level, combining elements of farming and fishing in their daily work. The linguistic results of this retention and its collapse will be discussed in Chapter 5.

1.3 Geography and culture: an introduction

1.3.1 The North-East

The North-East of Scotland consists of a coastal strip of low-lying land with higher land the further south-west you travel. The low-lying land

Map 2 The North-East of Scotland

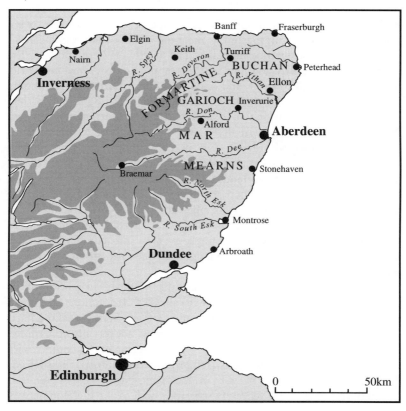

is generally very fertile, particularly in Kincardineshire, Angus and the Laigh (/lex/), 'low-lying part', of Moray. In the areas of the territory which are hilly, but not necessarily mountainous, there has been a long-standing tradition of the husbanding of sheep and, in particular, cattle.

The North-East is geographically discrete from the rest of the mainland. Moving from the south up Strathmore, the first major barrier to northward movement is the complex of river valleys associated with the South Esk. At this point, travellers in the past would have been channelled towards the coast. At the coast, however, is the Montrose Basin, a large tidal basin which at high tide reaches almost six kilometres inland, but at low tide is almost empty, with treacherous sands exposed. At the mouth of the basin, the gap between north and south is only a matter of metres; when the tide is turning, however, the race would have made the crossing impossible before a bridge was built. Just to the north is the valley of the North Esk, which has, at times, an impressively deep valley.

Travellers from the south might have chosen to climb up the valleys of these rivers to reach passes through the mountains into the Dee valley. With one exception – the Fungle Road – all are high (sometimes close to 1,000 metres at their summits) and would have been impassable for a large part of the winter.

If a traveller had chosen to continue along Strathmore, the sea would be reached at Stonehaven. Here the traveller would have had to cross the Highland Boundary fault, either by taking the Slug Road, a relatively low pass into the heart of the North-East, or the Cossiemounth, a low-level walk across to Aberdeen.

These barriers to communication have meant that historically the Mearns has been associated more strongly with Angus to its south than with Aberdeen to its north. But Aberdeen itself provided a number of useful choices to travellers, because the rivers Dee and Don, both major arteries, reach the sea at this point.

Although the higher passes were used until the modern era to herd cattle towards the markets of southern Scotland, invaders who were intent on coming north of the Grampians generally crossed at the coast. The Roman forces of Agricola probably used this route in 83 or 84 CE; it was certainly the favoured route of English invaders from the Battle of Nechtansmere (685) on. The importance of this short stretch of low-lying land can be seen in the number of fortifications clustered to its south, the most famous of which being Dunnottar Castle.

North of the mountains, several provinces were recognised in the medieval period. The area around the Dee was Mar. The lower valley of the Don was the Garioch (/'giri/), the agricultural heartland of the area. Its chief town is Inverurie (/ɪnvər'uri/). Although close to Aberdeen, the hills between this fertile area and the city have meant that the Garioch has maintained its integrity better than many other areas in the North-East.

North of the river Ythan is Buchan (/ˈbʌxən/), largely made up of a plateau where cattle have traditionally been reared, with a coastal area associated strongly with fishing, particularly in Peterhead and Fraserburgh. The upper valley of the Ythan, centred on Fyvie (/ˈfaevi/), is often called the Formartine (/fɔrˈmartən/), and associated more with the Garioch than with Buchan.

The Deveron valley is a discrete unit. The upper valley is dominated by sheep and cattle rearing; its primary centre is Huntly. It can be reached from the Formartine through the Glens of Foudland. Better agricultural land is present the further north you travel down the river; the primary business of the north of Banffshire was fishing, however, particularly in Banff itself, Cullen and Gamrie (/ˈgemri/; officially, Gardenstown).

To the west of the Deveron, the coastal lowlands widen, particularly in the lower Spey valley: the Laigh of Moray. This area contains some of the best land in Scotland, and consists of towns such as Fochabers, Elgin and Forres, along with a number of fairly large agricultural villages. Fishing centres, including Buckie and Lossiemouth (currently housing a Royal Air Force base) lie along the coast. At the edge of the Laigh are a number of whisky-producing centres, including Keith and Dufftown. Although Moray is strongly associated with the North-East, the presence of the Spey valley, with its long fairly low-lying connections to both southern and western Scotland, has meant that the area has been more open to outside influence than has the rest of the territory.

West of Moray, the North-East could be said to 'peter out' in the neighbourhood of Nairn. This distinction is generally made on linguistic grounds since it is in this area that the boundary of the *Gaidhealtachd*, the Gaelic-speaking part of Scotland, reached the sea in the eighteenth century. Across the Beauly Firth from Nairn is the Black Isle.

Aberdeen has some 200,000 inhabitants. Unlike Glasgow in particular, however, its growth over the last few centuries has been steady rather than in spurts due to industrial development. That is not to say that Aberdeen did not have a strong industrial sector. Given that sheep farming in particular was much practised in its rural hinterland, it is not surprising that weaving was a trade of some importance in the city. But the lack of either coal or iron in the North-East meant that an 'industrial revolution' similar to that of central Scotland was not possible.

Instead, Aberdeen acted as a major market for the agricultural produce of its hinterland, as well as becoming, with the advent of the railway, a major conduit for livestock being sent to the south. A fishing port in its own right, the city also acted as a trading port for the whole of the region, involved with other traders across the North Sea and into the Baltic since at least the late middle ages. This association with long-distance commerce led to the development of secondary trades such as shipbuilding, which were particularly profitable when wood was the preferred raw material. Aberdeen remains a major artery of ferry transport to the Northern Isles, which has more recently been supplemented by the presence of an international airport.

In recent years the Aberdeen area has become intimately connected with the exploitation of North Sea oil. As well as giving the inhabitants of the city considerable affluence at a period when farming and, in particular, fishing were in decline, this led to mass immigration from many other parts of the English-speaking world and elsewhere. The linguistic consequences of these changes are discussed in Chapter 5.

1.3.2 The Black Isle

The Black Isle (actually a peninsula) lies between the Beauly (/ˈbjuli/) and Cromarty Firths. Its history can be interpreted as largely the result

Map 3 The Black Isle and surroundings

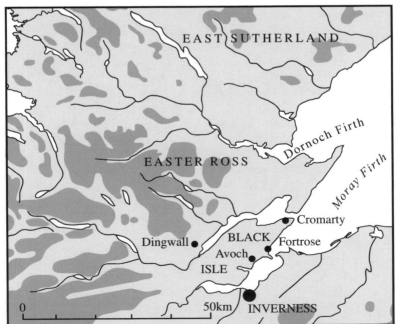

of its relatively cut-off nature, its generally fertile soil and dry climate, and its long coastline with several good harbours, the most important of which being Fortrose and Avoch (to the south) and Cromarty (to the north). The particular distinctiveness of the fishing communities had, as we will see, a linguistic dimension.

1.3.3 Caithness

Caithness consists mainly of a largely treeless plateau sloping north-wards and eastwards towards the sea. While some of the plateau is used for arable farming, most land is marginal and mainly employed for live-stock rearing. To the south lie mountains. Communication along the east coast is difficult even today at the Ord of Caithness. The subsequent descent to sea level and immediate precipitate ascent of the Berriedale Braes is formidable. Although communication is not as difficult to the west, Caithness still feels separate from its highland neighbours.

A large part of the coastline of the county is cliff, with abundant bird life. The two main centres of population in the county – Wick on the

Map 4 Caithness

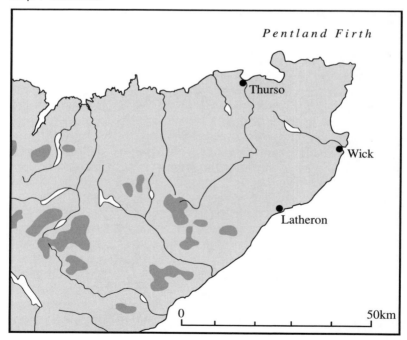

east coast and Thurso on the north – were major whaling and fishing centres until the twentieth century, acting as both home port and outfitter.

The trunk route A9 ends at Thurso. Nearby, at Scrabster, is the primary link from mainland Scotland to Orkney, through the ferry to Stromness. In recent years a ferry from John o'Groats (to the east of Thurso) to St Margaret's Hope on South Ronaldsay has also been introduced.

1.3.4 The Orkney Isles

The Orkneys have been inhabited for at least 3,000 years, and very likely for considerably longer. Many of the islands in the archipelago contain excellent farming land. Livestock – in particular the rearing of sheep for both wool and food – has long been part of the islands' economy. The proximity of the sea to almost all inhabitants of the islands (as well as, in the case of the Mainland, the most central and largest island in the archipelago, of both seawater and freshwater lochs) means that fish and shellfish were always available. There are highland districts, in particular on Hoy, but even these more marginal areas were useful for the harvesting of peat. This is particularly important for islands where there has been little native woodland for centuries.

Until recently a large part of the population was employed in a combined cultivation of smallholdings and inshore fishing. The partial exceptions to this were the inhabitants of the two main towns, Kirkwall (the capital) and Stromness, both on the coast of the Mainland, the latter facing south towards Scotland, the former facing north.

Another fundamental feature of the islands is the large expanse of sheltered water, called Scapa Flow, between the islands of Hoy, Flotta, South Ronaldsay, Burray and the Mainland. This harbour was used by military and merchant vessels for centuries. Possible linguistic consequences of this presence will be discussed in Chapter 5.

Unlike Shetland, Orkney is close to the Scottish mainland. For as far back as we have records, there have been close connections with Caithness in particular. Although we should not downplay its Scandinavian heritage, Orkney has been affected intimately by the social, political and economic changes which have affected the Scottish mainland in recent centuries. There have inevitably been linguistic consequences of this intimacy.

Like many 'marginal' areas, Orkney suffered from poverty and depopulation in the modern age. This was partly stemmed by the development of

Map 5 Orkney

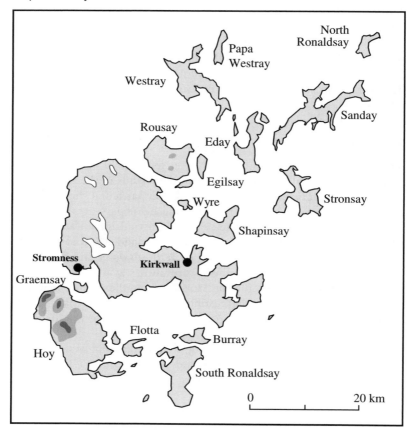

oil-based industries in the islands from the late 1960s on. Perhaps most striking was the development of almost all of Flotta as an oil and gas processing complex connected to many of the central oilfields in the North Sea. Potential linguistic results of these great changes will be discussed in Chapter 5.

1.3.5 Shetland

Many of the observations made for Orkney can also be made for Shetland. Both have been inhabited for lengthy periods and possess a rich archaeological heritage; both were settled by 'Picts' who were conquered culturally and linguistically by Scandinavian settlers; both had until

Map 6 Shetland

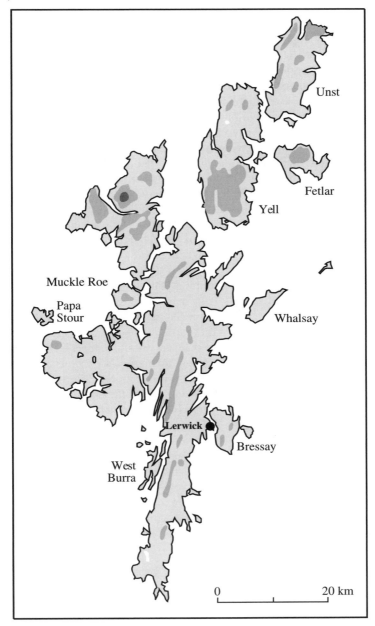

Unst

Fetlar

Yell

Muckle Roe

Papa
Stour

Whalsay

Lerwick

Bressay

West
Burra

0   20 km

relatively recently an economy based upon near-subsistence level farming and fishing. A number of differences exist between the island chains, however.

The most notable of these is geographical. While Orkney is visible from the Scottish mainland, Shetland is much further away. Given its situation, we might have expected Shetland to remain within the orbit of Norway or Denmark, perhaps following the same path towards autonomy as its relatively close neighbour the Faeroes. This is not the case due to medieval Shetland's subordinate position in the Earldom of Orkney.

Moreover, while Orkney consists largely of islands of similar size, with even the mainland having only roughly twice the surface area of the larger islands, Shetland is dominated by its mainland, with even the larger islands representing only a fraction of the mainland's surface area. While the distances between the different islands of Orkney are relatively small, some of the Shetland archipelago – Foula and Fair Isle in particular – lie considerable distances from the mainland. Until the advent of air travel, they could be cut off from the rest of Shetland for considerable periods.

These geographical realities have linguistic repercussions.

Shetland has always been more dependent upon fishing than farming. Although there is some good farming land, the red sandstone basis for Orkney's agricultural success is in marked contrast with the thin soils standing on a largely schist base in Shetland. Moreover, if nowhere in Orkney is far from the sea, this is even more the case with Shetland. Parts of the mainland are little more than an isthmus between the Atlantic Ocean and the North Sea; this is even more marked with some of the other settled areas, such as the Out Skerries. The position of the archipelago in relatively deep and cold waters has led to the inhabitants being involved in both inshore and deep sea fishing. It has also attracted fishermen and fishing entrepreneurs from elsewhere in Europe for centuries.

As with Orkney, North Sea oil brought with it considerable opportunities along with problems of various sorts. A major base for the oil industry was established at Sullom Voe. Direct injections of oil-based cash into the local economy helped at least to slow down rural depopulation and encourage the local culture; on the other hand, there was a large influx of both temporary and long-term resident outsiders. Again, these events have affected local language use.

1.4 A note on terminology: 'Scots' versus 'English'

You may have noticed that I rarely call the varieties we will look at in this book 'dialects of English'. This may appear strange to many of you, particularly since this book forms a part of a series termed just that. I have done this, however, because the Germanic dialects of Scotland are in some ways socially, historically and culturally different from the other descendants of Old English. Primarily this is due to the fact that by the time printing technology became widely available in the British Isles, Standard English was practically the only dialect of English employed with the new technology in England. In Scotland, however, the separate political tradition meant that the local varieties *were* regularly employed in print. Indeed, the Edinburgh variety of Scots was developing towards being the official language of the Scottish state in the middle of the sixteenth century. If England and Scotland had not become united under the same monarchy (in 1603) and parliament (in 1707), it is very likely that Scots and English would now be considered as separate (but closely related) languages in the same way as modern German and Dutch are.

Although this early modern autonomy was eventually lost, with Scots being *dialectalised* as a part of English, the primary language of literacy for all Scots-speakers, Scots has been maintained as a literary language which acts as a national symbol for many people. In a sense, English is external to Scotland in a way not possible for the rest of the English-speaking world (further discussion of these points can be found in Millar [2005]).

1.5 Conclusion

In the following chapters, many of the points made here will be returned to. In Chapter 2, the phonological variation in the area will be discussed; Chapter 3 focuses on the morphosyntax of the dialects; and Chapter 4 will discuss the lexical use. In Chapter 5, we will return to the linguistic history of the region, paying particular attention to the effects of language contact and language shift.

2 Phonetics and phonology

2.1 Introduction

When dealing with Scottish dialects, it must always be remembered that while it suits language activists to treat Scots and Standard English as separate languages, and the speech of many Scots may not be readily intelligible to English speakers who do not live in Scotland, most people regularly blend SSE and local dialect features in their everyday speech. This state of affairs is a relatively recent arrival to the Northern Isles and the northern mainland, and may, as we will see in Chapter 5, differ from place to place, but it is nonetheless present. Some people may rarely employ the word to sound correspondences of their local dialect; they will nevertheless come into daily contact with other locals who do. The relationship of the local Scots dialects and SSE is one of mutual interpenetration.

In addition to this, as we have already noted, a great many – probably the vast majority of – people local to these regions will not keep their local phonological system and that of SSE entirely apart. This works in two ways: there is regular 'seepage' from the SSE pattern into the local one; the opposite tendency is also present, of course.

Many speakers will employ local phonological patterns when they are self-consciously speaking English. For instance, it is quite common to hear, particularly in the speech of older people in Aberdeen, *bother* being pronounced /ˈbʌðər/, even when the rest of their discourse may be conducted entirely according to the phonological pattern of SSE. On the other hand, I regularly hear local young people here in Aberdeen speaking dense local dialect who will say *fit* /fɪt/ for 'what', but /ˈmɔtɪvər/ (perhaps even /ˈwɔtɪvər/) for 'whatever', particularly as a marker of disdain, apathy or lack of interest, a usage which appears to have largely been borrowed directly from American popular culture (indeed, I regularly hear, particularly in the speech of young women, a voicing of the medial /t/, a marked American feature which is otherwise unknown in local speech).

Figure 2.1 The vowel phonemes of SSE, Received Pronunciation and General American (after Abercrombie 1979: 72; modified). RP /ɜː/ is not represented here, since it occurs only before /r/. All three varieties also have /ə/. Its use in stressed contexts in Caithness dialect will be discussed in 2.2.3.6, 2.2.3.8 and 2.2.3.9 below.

	SSE	RP	GenAm
bead	*1* i	*1* iː	*1* iː
bid	*2* ɪ	*2* ɪ	*2* ɪ
bay	*3* e	*3* eɪ	*3* eɪ
bed	*4* ɛ	*4* ɛ	*4* ɛ
bad	*5* a	*5* a	*5* æ
balm		*6* ɑː	*6* ɑː
not	*8* ɔ	*7* ɒ	
nought		*8* ɔː	*8* ɔː
no	*9* o	*9* əʊ	*9* oʊ
pull	*11* u	*10* ʊ	*10* ʊ
pool		*11* uː	*11* uː
bud	*12* ʌ	*12* ʌ	*12* ʌ
side	*13* əi	*14* aɪ	*14* aɪ
sighed	*14* ae		
now	*15* əu	*15* aʊ	*15* aʊ
boy	*16* ɔe	*16* ɔɪ	*16* ɔɪ

Indeed, the importance of SSE as an alternative system employing essentially the same phonemes must be borne in mind for all these dialects: in the process of learning to read, if not earlier, speakers of local dialects are introduced to this alternative attribution system. Its relationship to the phonemes of Received Pronunciation (RP) and General American (GenAm) can be illustrated as above.

Even before we begin a discussion of local pronunciations within northern Scotland and the Northern Isles, we can see that a specifically Scottish pronunciation pattern is present, distinct from both dominant pronunciations (RP and GenAm). Part of this distinction is due to perceptions of vowel length.

2.1.1 Scottish vowel length

Historically, all Germanic languages distinguished between vowels of the same *quality* (the position of the tongue and lips) by means of *quantity* (the duration of the vowel). Most Scottish people today are largely unaware of vowel quantity, concentrating on the *quality* of the vowels. Thus, when an RP speaker says /bɑ:θ/, 'bath', in comparison to /kat/, 'cat', a distinction all but the most upper-middle-class or upper-class Scottish speakers do not make, many Scots would interpret the back quality of /ɑ:/ as what distinguishes it from /a/, rather than length. The historical length of vowels has been almost entirely superseded by vowel length based solely upon the environment in which a vowel is placed. Thus some historically long vowels have a short realisation in Scottish speech, while maintaining, more often than not, a similar quality to their long variants. For instance, the vowel in *seed* is short, while that in *he* is long.

Lengthening or shortening of a vowel according to environmental constraints is by no means uncommon in English as a whole. What marks off Scottish accents (and also some accents from the North East of England) as being 'unusual' is the extent to which these processes are thoroughgoing, so that we can speak of a *Scottish Vowel-length Rule*, as proposed by Aitken (1981), and discussed in some detail by Abercrombie (1979).

According to this rule, vowels are long when they are (1) in morpheme-final position,

Figure 2.2 Scottish Vowel Length Rule 1

Long		Short	
sea	[si:]	seed	[sid]
lay	[le:]	late	[let]
coup	[ku:]	coop	[kup]
rye	[rae]	rite	[rəit]
how	[hʌ:u]	howl	[həul]
Heh! (expression of greeting, surprise)	[hɛ:]	head	[hɛd]
Da (affectionate name for a father)	[da:]	Dad	[dad]

(2) followed by /v, ð, z, r/ :

Figure 2.3 Scottish Vowel Length Rule 2

Long		Short	
Beith (town in Ayrshire)	[biːð]	Beath (town in Fife)	[biθ]
haze	[heːz]	haste	[hest]
poor	[puːr]	put	[put]
live (not recorded)	[laev]	life	[ləif]
lour	[ləːur]	lout	[ləut]
berth	[bɛːrθ]	Beth (pet form of Elizabeth)	[bɛθ]
vase	[vaːz]	vassal	['vasl]

or (3), followed by an inflectional suffix:

Figure 2.4 Scottish Vowel Length Rule 3

Long		Short	
peas	[piːz]	Pisa	['pizə]
played	[pleːd]	blade	[bled]
renewed	[rɪ'njuːd]	new	[nju]
tied	[taed]	tide	[təid]
cowed	[kəːud]	coward	['kəuərd]
said	[sɛːd]	bed	[bɛd]
mas (a group of mothers)	[maːz]	mass	[mas]

A number of points should be noted about the rule. First, there are some situations where it does not apply in any Scottish variety. Certain vowels, such as /ɔ/ (or, in some dialects, /a/) in words like *law* or /o/ in words like *throat* are always long, as is, often, the first element in the diphthong found in words like *choice*. There are a number of historical short vowels, such as /ɪ/ in words like *bit*, or /ʌ/ in words like *but*, which are always short. Furthermore, the duration of 'long' and 'short' vowels varies considerably between the vowels and between people (McClure 1977).

Second, and unusually, the vowel length rule also affects some of the diphthongs in Scottish speech. In the case of /əu/, it has to be recognised that the difference between long and short duration is barely perceptible. Much more striking is the distinction found between /ae/ and /əi/. The second diphthong is shorter in duration than the first; more importantly, this is the only example of the effects of the SVLR where the two variants are distinguished not only by quantity but also by quality. Wells (1982: II, 405–6) claims that the two vowels are allophones, since their use is environmentally conditioned, a point which seems to be supported by the evidence on vowel length given above. However, there is at least one minimal pair in Scots (rather than in SSE) which is not conditioned: *ay*, /ae/, 'yes', and *aye*, /əi/, 'always'.

Finally, the further north from central Scotland you travel, the more there will be specific words which do not conform to the rule. van Leyden (2004: 3.5) suggests that the duration of syllables in Shetland dialect is different from other Scots dialects and can plausibly be associated with the syllable duration of some Norwegian varieties.

2.2 The vowel systems

2.2.1 Lexical sets

Perhaps the single greatest contribution to our analysis of the vowel systems of varieties of English is that of Wells (1982). Using a group of headwords, which he felt best represented the potential distinctions in pronunciation between vowels in a particular part of the English-speaking world, Wells produced a number of *lexical sets* which provide a transparent means of analysing phonemic distinctions between varieties without becoming submerged in the actual quality (phonemic and, more challengingly, phonetic) of the vowels associated with a particular place.

This form of analysis works because it is almost always possible for any native speaker to analyse the pronunciation of a previously unknown variety relatively quickly due to a largely unconscious construction of patterns similar to these lexical sets.

Unfortunately, as can be seen in the following figures and discussion, Wells' attribution of words to lexical sets is not straightforward even when analysing the SSE distribution. It is much more problematical when we recognise that although SSE and Scots normally have the same set of vowels in any Scottish accent, the lexical sets associated with these sets of vowels are often strikingly different.

Because of this, I have largely followed the lexical sets of Johnson (1997), with the proviso that often the headwords of his lexical sets are given by Johnson in their Standard English form, requiring the reader to work out the Scots cognate. This is not always easy. For the sake of transparent comparison with Johnson's work, however, I have retained his headwords except where there is potential confusion over what sets of words are being foregrounded.

For instance, the vowel represented by BOOT in SSE is represented by OOT, 'out', in all varieties of Scots. In SSE, the OOT words would be part of the OUT diphthongal set (represented in Scots by LOWP, 'leap'). Moreover, the MATE set in SSE is considerably larger in all Scots varieties, since many SSE GOAT words are in this set for Scots. For that reason, I have renamed the SSE lexical set as MATE-HAME, the latter word being a particularly striking example of this distinction, since *hame* is the Scots cognate of English *home*. Finally, Scots has an extra lexical set, not found at all in SSE, which I have termed BUIT, 'boot'. This lexical set is merged with other lexical sets in most varieties of Scots. This is not the case with a number of the dialects under consideration in this book, however.

To demonstrate the correspondences between Wells' lexical sets and those Johnson proposes for the Scottish varieties, as emended by me, I present here a comparative diagram, demonstrating the lexical sets of SSE, following Johnson's attribution in relation to those which Wells proposes. In the central column are the lexical sets of the Scots dialects. The three lists are associated roughly by pronunciation, but not necessarily in terms of which words are found in which set (see figure 2.5).

It should be noted that there are very few, if any, dialects of Scots which maintain all these distinctions. It is possible, however, for each of these lexical sets to be immune from the mergers found in SSE in one dialect or another, however. What the normal distribution patterns of these lexical sets are will be discussed in the next section.

2.2.2 The monophthong patterns of SSE and Northern and Insular Scots: an introduction

In the following diagrams I have attempted to give a brief summary of how the vowel phonemes found in the dialects of Scots spoken in our region are distributed. They are intended to give you a fixed point around which all the following more detailed discussion revolves. It is very easy to become confused with the plethora of detail available for each dialect grouping, and even inside the larger groupings. It should be noted that all Scots dialects have four phonemic diphthongs: CHOICE, OWER, BITE and TRY. Because the distribution of these sets is fairly

Figure 2.5 Lexical sets used in this book compared to those of Wells (1982)

SSE	Scots	Wells (1982)
No equivalent	BUIT	*No equivalent*
MEET/BEAT	MEET	FLEECE
	BEAT	
MATE/BAIT	MATE-HAME	FACE
	BAIT	
DRESS	DRESS	DRESS
TRAP	TRAP	TRAP/BATH/PALM/START
KIT	KIT	KIT
STRUT	STRUT	STRUT
BOOT	OOT	FOOT/GOOSE/CURE
GOAT	GOAT	GOAT
CAUGHT/COT	CAUGHT	THOUGHT/NORTH
	COT	LOT/CLOTH
OUT	OWER	MOUTH
BITE	BITE	PRICE
TRY	TRY	
CHOICE	CHOICE	CHOICE

uniform in all Scots varieties (with the exceptions discussed below), I have only treated the monophthongs in this section.

Nevertheless, there are a number of points which should be noted before we take a look at the phonological systems. In the first place, it is important to recognise that they are broad-brush schematisations. There is, as we will see, considerable variation within the dialect areas, both between communities and across the social spectrum.

Perhaps most importantly, I have laid out the lexical sets in the diagrams according to a rough approximation of the vowel quadrilateral. While many speakers do pronounce the words of a particular lexical set (or combination of lexical sets) in places similar to what is laid out here, this need not be the case. For instance, the actual sound associated with the BOOT lexical set in SSE and the OOT lexical set in Scots can vary from back to centre to front in the various dialects discussed in this book, depending both on what particular dialect is represented and what the age of the speaker is. In addition, it should be remembered that there will be environments – perhaps most notably before /r/ or /n/ – where the vowel employed in a word may not be that expected for that set of spellings. A good example of this is the Scots equivalent to English *stone.* Most Central Scots dialects would include this word in the lexical set I term here MATE-HAME. In a number of the dialects discussed here – Mid-Northern A, some South Northern dialects, and Shetlandic – this word (and other MATE-HAME words where the vowel precedes /n/) have merged with MEET. Although this point is important, developing it further here would only confuse the large-scale discussion included in this section. It is better placed with our in-depth discussions below.

2.2.2.1 SSE

In SSE there are essentially nine contrastive lexical sets, one of which represents a merger between COT and CAUGHT. In Shetland, on the other hand, a rather different pattern is evident:

Figure 2.6 SSE monophthong pattern

MEET/ BEAT	KIT	BOOT
MATE/BAIT	STRUT	GOAT
		COT/CAUGHT
DRESS		
TRAP		

2.2.2.2 Shetlandic

Figure 2.7   Shetlandic monophthong pattern

BUIT		
MEET	KIT	OOT
BEAT/MATE-HAME/	STRUT	(GOAT)
BAIT/DRESS		(GOAT/CAUGHT/COT)
		(CAUGHT)
		(COT)
TRAP		

In the first place, the dialects of Shetland have maintained a distinction between BUIT and all other lexical sets. On the other hand BEAT, generally merged with MEET in SSE, is merged here with MATE-HAME, BAIT and DRESS. As is indicated by the brackets, some Shetland varieties maintain a distinction between GOAT, CAUGHT and COT, while others have merged all three sets. In SSE, of course, only CAUGHT and COT are merged.

2.2.2.3 Orcadian

Figure 2.8 Orcadian monophthong pattern

BUIT		
MEET	KIT	OOT
BEAT/MATE-HAME/BAIT/DRESS	STRUT	GOAT
		CAUGHT
		COT
TRAP		

Orkney dialects realise a very similar phonological pattern to the Shetland varieties although, as we will see, the completed merger between GOAT, CAUGHT and COT in some Shetland dialects is only a general tendency towards merger in the more southerly archipelago.

2.2.2.4 North Northern B (Caithness)

Figure 2.9 North Northern B monophthong pattern

BUIT/MEET	KIT	OOT
BEAT/MATE-HAME/	STRUT	GOAT
BAIT		CAUGHT
DRESS		
		COT
TRAP		

The phonological system of Caithness dialect contains a number of similarities to the Orkney dialects. For instance, the merger between BEAT, MATE-HAME and BAIT is similar to (although somewhat less extensive than) the systems of the Insular dialects. But it also shares many features with the other Northern dialects, however. This is most noticeable in the merger of BUIT with MEET.

2.2.2.5 North Northern A

Figure 2.10 North Northern A monophthong pattern

BUIT/MEET	KIT	OOT
BEAT/MATE-HAME/	STRUT	GOAT
BAIT		
		CAUGHT
DRESS		
		COT
TRAP		

Like Caithness, North Northern A has the typical Northern merger of BUIT and MEET and what could be seen as the North Northern merger of BEAT with MATE-HAME and BAIT.

2.2.2.6 Mid-Northern B

Figure 2.11 Mid-Northern B monophthong pattern

BUIT/MEET/BEAT	KIT	OOT
MATE-HAME	STRUT	GOAT
BAIT		CAUGHT
DRESS		
		COT
TRAP		

Mid-Northern B, however, has the expected merger of BUIT and MEET, but both merging with BEAT. MATE-HAME and BAIT remain separate both from this merger and each other, however. It is therefore similar to, but still distinct from, Mid-Northern A:

2.2.2.7 Mid-Northern A

Figure 2.12 Mid-Northern A monophthong pattern

BUIT/MEET/BEAT	KIT	OOT
MATE-HAME/BAIT/	STRUT	GOAT
DRESS		
		CAUGHT
		COT
TRAP		

Mid-Northern A has, like its more western counterpart, a merger of BUIT, MEET and BEAT. In this set of dialects, however, there is a common merger between MATE-HAME, BAIT and DRESS. In some ways, Mid-Northern A has the 'simplest' phoneme pattern of any of the dialects discussed in this book.

2.2.2.8 South Northern

Figure 2.13 South Northern monophthong pattern

(BUIT)		
(BUIT)/MEET/BEAT	KIT	OOT
(BUIT)/MATE-HAME/	STRUT	GOAT
(BAIT)		
(BAIT)		CAUGHT/COT
DRESS		
TRAP		

It is South Northern, in fact, where variation from the norm (or, perhaps better, variation between norms) is particularly widespread. We can see this most readily in the treatment of BUIT, which has a rounded pronunciation in some Angus varieties within this region. To some speakers, words forming part of this lexical set are pronounced with a vowel unique to it: this is similar to the Insular dialects, but unlike other mainland Scots varieties. To other speakers, BUIT words form part of a merger with MEET and BEAT: this is identical to the most common pattern found in the Northern area. Finally, some speakers would place BUIT in a merger with at least MATE-HAME and possibly also BAIT. This pattern has some similarities with the common reflexes of BUIT found in the Mid-Scots dialects, but is distinct from them.

Moreover, to some speakers, many of the words which form part of BAIT would be pronounced the same as MATE-HAME words, while other speakers would distinguish between BAIT and MATE-HAME on most occasions. The former merger is the norm in more southern parts of Scotland, but is less common the further north you travel. Most South Northern speakers also merge COT and CAUGHT, but not necessarily GOAT, another point where features are shared with some of the Northern Isles varieties and also Central Scots dialects.

2.2.2.1 Discussion

Even with this brief treatment, we can see patterns emerging between the dialects. South Northern shares features with the Insular dialects, Mid-Northern and, to a lesser extent, North Northern. Mid-Northern A seems to be more radical than Mid-Northern B, if we assume that the mergers involved are what they appear: a union of previously separate lexical sets. It might even be suggested that Mid-Northern A is the centre of change for a large part of the areas covered in this book.

What we need to do now, however, is consider the more detailed distribution of these lexical sets in the areas under discussion. This will help us see whether these patterns – and others – are still remarkable at a smaller scale.

2.2.3 *The vowel phonology of the dialect areas*

In the following discussion, each lexical set will be treated independently (although, as we have already noted, there are practically no places in the Northern and Insular Scots-speaking areas where all the possible elements are realised as such). It should be noted that I am concerned here primarily with stressed vowels. In recent years Fitzgerald (2002) and Paster (2004) have discussed the phonology of unstressed vowels in

Mid-Northern A, as with the second /ɪ/ in /nɪvɪr/ 'never' with what appears to be vowel harmony. Because of the complexity of their findings (from the point of view of readers who are not specialists in either phonetics or phonology), their findings will not be incorporated here. It is to be hoped, however, that more work of this type will be undertaken in the future.

With each lexical set we will deal in the first place with the Northern dialects, moving outward from Mid-Northern A. This will be followed by discussion of the Insular Scots varieties. Each of these sub-sections are preceded by a table summarising the main points made.

2.2.3.1 BUIT, 'boot'
2.2.3.1.1 Northern Scots

Figure 2.14 BUIT in Northern Scots

BUIT	
MNA	Merger with MEET, except *school, good, cool*: /wi/ *Foot* merged with KIT
MNB	Merger with MEET, except *school, good, cool*: /wi/ *Foot* merged with KIT
NNA	Merger with MEET *Foot* merged with KIT
NNB	Merger with MEET *Foot* merged with KIT
SN	Some merger with MEET; merger with MATE-HAME in south Kincardineshire and Angus Western Angus /y/ *Foot* merged with KIT

In Mid- and North Northern Scots /i/ is realised for BUIT, so that *moon* is /min/, *spoon* /spin/, *boot* /bit/, and so on. SSE /u/ is generally found before /v/, /ð/ and /z/ (Johnston 1997: 466), so that words such as *move, prove* and *smooth* are part of OOT. Exceptions to this are *sure, use* (verb), *confuse* and (with very elderly speakers) *bruise*, pronounced with /i/ in traditional Mid- and North Northern Scots. /i/ is also regular when BUIT is followed by /r/, so that *poor* (pronounced /pur/ in SSE) is /pir/ and *floor* /flir/. *Pour*, on the other hand, is pronounced either /por/ or, often, /pur/.

In traditional Mid-Northern dialects, a preceding velar plosive triggers a following /w/, so that the equivalent of *good* is /gwid/, *school* /skwil/ and *cool* /kwil/. It is in these contexts, despite their distinctiveness (and the status of spellings such as *gweed* or *skweel* as markers of local identity), that the /i/ pronunciation is perhaps most under stress. This particular sub-set does not exist in North Northern.

Hook and *poor* and similar words often have /ju/ in Morayshire and North Northern, but these are gradually being replaced with the Standard /u/. /ju/ is retained for some speakers of Mid-Northern A with *heuk*, 'sickle', but not *hook* on a fishing line, however. The /ju/ has also been retained in the name of the River Feugh – /fjux/ – in Kincardineshire.

The South Northern situation is complex. In Angus, the prevailing BUIT pronunciation is /e/, often merged with BEAT, when members of that set are pronounced /e/. Using /e/ in all BUIT contexts is unique to this area, although Central Scots varieties often have that sound before /r/, as in *puir* /per/, 'poor'. Some traditional West Angus speakers retain /y/ in these contexts (a feature they share with Insular varieties). Many traditional speakers from Kincardineshire follow the Mid-Northern pattern for BUIT, with /i/ in most contexts and /wi/ following a velar plosive. On this occasion, the area is overtly a transition zone.

In all of these dialects, a single exception to the local pronunciation is found with the equivalent of English *foot*, which is always pronounced /fɪt/. This is the normal pronunciation in Central Scots, and was probably incorporated in the Northern dialects to avoid confusion between *foot* and *feet*.

2.2.3.1.2 *Insular Scots*

Figure 2.15 BUIT in Insular Scots

BUIT	
Shetland	/y/ *foot* merged with KIT
Orkney	/y/, except *foot* *foot* merged with KIT Stronsay: merger with KIT; merger with MATE-HAME before /r/ and finally

In traditional Insular Scots the realisation of BUIT tends to be a high or high-mid fronted (or, in the case of west Shetland [Johnston 1997: 466], central to front) rounded vowel of the type [yɵʏ]. People from Stronsay in Orkney are the exception, however (ibid.: 466). They employ a pattern which is nearly identical with the most common pattern in Mid-Scots. Thus the equivalent of *moon* is /mɪn/, but of *do* /de/.

Orkney varieties in particular use /u/ in many contexts; this probably represents a borrowing from SSE. As with Moray and Caithness, BUIT before /p/ (*hoop*) and to a lesser extent /k/ (*look, book*) is likely to have /u/, replacing earlier /ju/.

In Shetland, the local orthography represents BUIT by <ö>.

2.2.3.2 MEET

2.2.3.2.1 Northern Scots

Figure 2.16 MEET in Northern Scots

MEET	
MNA	Generally merger with BUIT Generally merger with BEAT *die, fly, lie, king, wet, change* *clean* *stane* 'stone'
MNB	Generally merger with BUIT Generally merger with BEAT *die, fly, lie, king, wet, change* *clean*
NNA	Generally merger with BUIT Some merger with BEAT *die, fly, lie, wet* *clean* Nairn: *kick*
NNB	Some merger with BEAT *die, fly, lie, king, kick, swim, wet, change* *clean*
SN	Generally merger with BEAT *die, fly, lie, wet, change* *clean* *stane* 'stone'

In Northern dialects, the most common reflex of <ee> is /i/. There is some evidence (Johnston 1997: 455–6) that this monophthong replaced an earlier diphthong. For instance, in traditional Caithness dialect a diphthong [ɪi] is the norm in all contexts. The extent to which this diphthong represents a phonemic split from /i/ is dubious, but local people are certainly aware of their 'peculiarity'. In traditional Mid-Northern areas, diphthongal pronunciations for MEET are only common following historical /w/ or /ʍ/ in words such as *wet* (often /wit/ in Scotland), *weep, wheel, wheen,* 'a great deal', or *queen* (ibid.: 455). Older speakers in Moray are particularly aware of their diphthongal usage in comparison with the monophthongal pronunciations of Aberdeenshire.

The older diphthongal pronunciation may provide an origin for the common Mid-Northern word *quine,* 'girl', largely unknown elsewhere in Scotland. This word could be equivalent to English *queen,* although a more persuasive argument could be made for its being cognate to (obsolescent) *quean,* 'young woman (of dubious reputation)'. There is a tendency for the introduction of a very marked /ə/ after /i/ before /r/, in words such as *here.* While this distinction is phonetic for native speakers, it may seem phonemic to outsiders.

In Mid-Northern, *change* is pronounced /tʃindʒ/, and is therefore merged with MEET. *Clean* is also merged with MEET in all Northern Scots dialects, no matter how BEAT is normally pronounced in that dialect. *Die, fly* and *lie* are also often pronounced with /i/, as is *wet.*

In some of these dialects, words which have /ɪ/ in SSE have /i/. This is most common with *king* /kiŋ/. The process is particularly widespread in Caithness. We will discuss this phenomenon more when we deal with KIT words. On the other hand, there is also a tendency towards a /ɪ/, rather than /i/ pronunciation before /k/ with some MEET words. In the North-East, *week* is /wɪk/. The BEAT word *speak* is also regularly merged with KIT.

2.2.3.2.2 Insular Scots

Figure 2.17 MEET in Insular Scots

MEET	
Shetland	Some merger with BEAT *die, fly, lie* *clean* *stane* 'stone' Fair Isle: *egg*
Orkney	Some merger with BEAT *die, fly, lie, king, kick, swim* *clean* *stane* 'stone'

In the Northern Isles, MEET is generally /i/. Johnston (1997: 455) reports that 'there are some cases of unraised [e] before labials in the northernmost dialects', so that *heel* and *hale* may be homophones. Orcadian shares many features with Caithness dialect; in particular, the use of /i/ with a number of KIT words. Both archipelagos have merger of *stane* with MEET. *Die, fly, lie* and *clean* are also members of this set. *Egg* is traditionally a member of MEET on Fair Isle. We will look at this merger again with DRESS.

As in Northern Scots, words such as *week* and *speak* are regularly transferred to KIT. This phenomenon is most widespread in Shetland.

2.2.3.3 BEAT

2.2.3.3.1 Northern Scots

Figure 2.18 BEAT in Northern Scots

BEAT	
MNA	Generally merger with MEET; some merger with MATE-HAME
MNB	Generally merger with MEET; some merger with MATE-HAME
NNA	Generally merger with MATE-HAME; some merger with MEET
NNB	Generally merger with MATE-HAME; some merger with MEET
SN	Generally merger with MEET; some merger with MATE-HAME South Kincardineshire and Angus: *dyke*

The Northern Scots dialects are divided between those which have a general merger between BEAT and MATE-HAME and those which have a merger between BEAT with MEET (as is the case in SSE, of course).

The first merger is general in North Northern, as a diphthong [ɛi]. This diphthong is perceived by native speakers as being separate from the diphthong /əi/ in BITE (Johnston 1997: 457). The traditional dialects of southern parts of South Northern often have merger between BEAT and MATE-HAME. Many younger speakers can be heard having the more mainstream merger of BEAT with MEET, perhaps under the influence of the speech of Dundee and the Central Belt in general.

In Mid-Northern A and the northern parts of South Northern, the merger of BEAT with MEET is the norm, overwhelmingly at /i/, so that *bean* is /bin/. In the coastal dialects of Banffshire, northern Aberdeenshire and the northern parts of South Northern, however, BEAT merges with MATE-HAME in words such as *beat* /bet/ and *meat*

/met/, 'food' (ibid.: 457). Indeed, I have heard elderly South Northern speakers make a distinction between /met/, 'food', and /mit/, 'meat', where the latter may be a borrowing from SSE. In some varieties, the former has become associated almost entirely with animal – particularly dog – food; the latter with human food.

Merger, or near-merger, of BEAT and MATE-HAME is also common in traditional Moray coastal dialects. Other varieties of Mid-Northern B have merger with MEET in all contexts, however. The pattern of BEAT and MATE-HAME merger in Mid-Northern A and B suggests that this feature is particularly associated with the dialects of people who, at least until recently, were closely connected to the fishing trade.

In general, all <ea> words, no matter their SSE pronunciation, are pronounced as the majority of BEAT forms are in that area. Thus, in Mid-Northern A, *head*, *bread* and *dead* are all pronounced with /i/ rather than /ɛ/; this even extends to words which are not spelled <ea>, such as *well*, the adverbial equivalent of *good*, pronounced /wil/. In the southern dialects of South Northern, on the other hand, *head* and *dead* are often pronounced /hed/ and /ded/, particularly in the speech of older people or those who work, or have a background, in the agricultural industries.

Clean is pronounced with /i/ in all Northern Scots varieties, however, while *death* and *breath* are pronounced with the local MATE-HAME realisation – normally as /e/. Some older Mid-Northern A speakers would pronounce *death* as /did/.

/i/ is found in all Northern Scots varieties when the BEAT vowel is in final position (ibid.: 457), so that *lea*, 'leave, go away', is always /li/. *Tea* is often pronounced /te/, however, by elderly people from the fishing villages and towns of Buchan, especially in *shallie o tay*, 'shell [i.e. cup] of tea'. This may be maintained as a marker of local identity.

In traditional dialects, *sweat*, pronounced /swit/ in more southerly dialects, is pronounced /swəit/, merging with the BITE set. *Great* also takes part in this merger. Older speakers would regularly pronounce this word /grəit/.

2.2.3.3.2 *Insular Scots*

Figure 2.19 BEAT in Insular Scots

BEAT	
Shetland	Generally merger with MATE-HAME; some merger with MEET
Orkney	Generally merger with MATE-HAME; some merger with MEET

In Insular Scots, <ea> words are generally merged with MATE-HAME, at a somewhat low /e/, often retracted or diphthongised in Shetland, but monophthongal in Orkney (Johnston 1997: 457). *Read* (present tense) is regularly a homophone of *raid*, for instance. As in Northern Scots, the vowel in *clean* is /i/; outlying varieties also pronounce *heal* as /hil/.

2.2.3.4 MATE-HAME

2.2.3.4.1 Northern Scots

Figure 2.20 MATE-HAME in Northern Scots

MATE-HAME	
MNA	Merger with BAIT and DRESS Some palatalisation before or after velars: see TRAP
MNB	*stane* 'stone', *clathes* 'clothes' Some palatalisation before or after velars: see TRAP
NNA	Generally merger with BAIT and BEAT *stane* 'stone', *pay*
NNB	Merger with BAIT and BEAT by some speakers *stane* 'stone', *clathes* 'clothes' *pay*
SN	Incomplete merger with BAIT Merger with BUIT in south Kincardineshire and most of Angus *clathes* 'clothes'

In Mid-Northern A, there is generally merger between this set and BAIT and DRESS, whether as a monophthongal [e] (somewhat lower than that found to the south) or, in the coastal areas of Banffshire and western Aberdeenshire, an ingliding diphthong [eɛ] (ibid.: 460). The further west you travel, however, the more likely it is that MATE-HAME will be distinguished from BAIT, with the latter often being realised somewhat lower in the mouth, perhaps as /ɛ/ or as a diphthong, in at least the Moray varieties of Mid-Northern B.

In North Northern Scots, MATE-HAME, BAIT and BEAT are pronounced in similar, often identical, manners, with the exceptions mentioned in our discussion of BEAT above. Speakers in some parts of Caithness distinguish between the three. This may be the older pattern.

In the southern dialects of South Northern, there is generally a merger between MATE-HAME and BEAT. There is also some merger with BAIT, but this is not complete, particularly in Kincardineshire and the northern parts of Angus, where the three sets are, like some Caithness varieties, distinguished by similar, but not entirely identical, pronunciations (ibid.: 460).

As we saw with the BEAT words, there are sporadic mergers between BEAT and particular MATE-HAME words in most dialects, even when BEAT is normally pronounced /i/.

In all of the dialects, *make* and *take* are regularly /mak/ and /tak/, although the SSE pronunciations, /mek/ and /tek/, can be heard in even the most 'dense' dialect. *Twa*, 'two', is not /twe/, as we might expect, but actually /twa/, and therefore a member of TRAP.

In a similar way, some words which are part of MATE-HAME in SSE and many Central Scots dialects are not found in MATE-HAME in some Northern dialects.

Particularly in Aberdeenshire, a following velar – especially /k/ – may cause the substitution of /ja/ for /e/, so that *bake* and *cake* are pronounced /bjak/ and /kjak/ by speakers of traditional dialect, thus forming a sub-set of TRAP.

In Mid-Northern A, MATE-HAME vowels before /n/ merge with MEET, so the cognate of English *stone* is /stin/. In Mid-Northern B and South Northern, however, no such merger takes place, and the pronunciation of Scots *stane*, 'stone' is the expected /sten/. This development also affects the numeral *one*, although on this occasion traditional South Northern varieties have the apparently Mid-Northern /in/ rather than the expected /en/. /en/ is common in Mid-Northern B, however, where it may act as a marker of local identity in distinction to Mid-Northern A.

Diphthongal pronunciations are sometimes heard in Northern Scots for words pronounced with /e/ in SSE or Central Scots. *Wame*, 'belly', the Scots equivalent of *womb*, is /wəim/ throughout the Northern Scots area (merged with BITE). This change is confined to Mid-Northern A in other contexts following /w/, so that *wale*, 'choose', is there a homophone of *wile*, or /l/, most noticeably in the equivalent of mainstream Scots *cla(th)es*, 'clothes', pronounced /kləiz/ even when no other word of this type is transferred to BITE.

Caithness speech typically has a phonetically diphthongal realisation for MATE-HAME, although this is not merged with BITE. Native speakers seem particularly aware of this feature; it is regularly represented in dialect literature.

In North Northern, MATE-HAME before /r/ will regularly be lowered, so that *mare*, 'more', and *mare*, 'female adult horse', are /mɛr/. Lowering also happens in Mid-Northern A, although two syllable pronunciations with a semivocalic glide, such as ['mejər], are more common. Whether this represents an actual phonemic distinction depends upon whether the listener is a native or an incomer. It is a feature which Mid-Scots speakers reproduce when attempting impersonations of 'Doric' speech. Lowering to /mɛr/ is also occasionally heard in the more southern dialects of South Northern.

2.2.3.4.2 Insular Scots

Figure 2.21 MATE-HAME in Insular Scots

MATE-HAME	
Shetland	Generally merger with BAIT and BEAT *clathes* 'clothes' Whalsay: some palatalisation after velars: /je/ in *cake*
Orkney	Generally merger with BAIT and BEAT *clathes* 'clothes' Stronsay *do; floor*

In Insular Scots, patterns similar to the more conservative varieties of Northern Scots apply. MATE-HAME merges with BEAT in most environments, in whatever pronunciation BEAT has in that place (Johnston 1997: 459). Before or after velars or /r/, however, MATE-HAME merges with BAIT, so that *gate* or *sair* 'sore, painful' are pronounced differently from *late* and *sale*. As with Northern Scots A and many Mid-Northern varieties, MATE-HAME is pronounced /i/ before /n/ in words like /stin/ 'stone'. But while the pronunciation /in/ for 'one' is present in both archipelagos, a pronunciation /wan/ is also possible (ibid.: 459). There is some evidence for diphthongisation of *wame*, as in North Northern varieties, in at least some dialects.

In Whalsay in particular a /j/ glide develops with this vowel following /k/. *Cake* may therefore be /kjek/. Local speakers hear this initial palatalised consonant as /tʃ/, although phonetically it may approach [ç].

On the island of Stronsay in Orkney, BUIT vowels before /r/ or at the end of the word are merged with MATE-HAME, so that the equivalent of *floor* is /fler/, and of *do*, /de/. This is the same distribution found in Central Scots dialects.

2.2.3.5 BAIT

2.2.3.5.1 Northern Scots
In Northern Scots, 'the more peripheral a Northern dialect is, the more environments a separate BAIT reflex appears in' (Johnston 1997: 464).

Figure 2.22 BAIT in Northern Scots

BAIT	
MNA	Merged with MATE-HAME and DRESS
MNB	Generally merger with MATE-HAME, DRESS
NNA	Generally merger with MATE-HAME, BEAT
NNB	Merger with MATE-HAME and BEAT by some speakers
SN	Kincardineshire: generally merger with MATE-HAME, BAIT Angus: BAIT distinguished from MATE-HAME

Generally a merger between MATE-HAME and BAIT takes place in the 'centre' of Mid-Northern A, except where a diphthong develops in words such as *rain* and *tail*; this is at least similar to the vowel found in these contexts (and also with MATE-HAME and BAIT) before /r/, as in *pair*, /'pejər/.

Elsewhere in Mid-Northern, BAIT is distinct from MATE-HAME, generally as a vowel (whether monophthongal or diphthongal) somewhat lower than /e/, except when the BAIT vowel is followed by /s/, where merger with MATE-HAME takes place. Thus the vowel in *lay* may well be pronounced differently from that in *lace*.

As with most Scots dialects, there is a sub-set of BAIT where a diphthong is always present. Unlike many dialects of Scots, however, the equivalent of English *way* is pronounced not like BITE, but rather TRY, so that *whit wey*, 'why, for what reason', pronounced /ʍɪt wəi/ in Central Scots, is /fɪt wae/ (with a back [ɑ] first nucleus in the diphthong) in Mid-Northern.

Angus is very similar to Moray, with a distinction normally between MATE-HAME and BAIT. Unlike the periphery of Mid-Northern, large parts of Kincardineshire and northern Angus do not have diphthongal pronunciations for *rain* and *tail*, however. Like Mid-Northern, *pay* and *change* are realised with /ae/ and /i/ respectively. *Way*, on the other hand, is pronounced as TRY well into northern Angus, but with BITE to the south (the Mid-Scots realisation).

Some – particularly younger – speakers of North Northern, along with the fisher folk of Thurso, merge BAIT with MATE-HAME and BEAT. Those living furthest from the centres of population, particularly if they are older, generally maintain a distinction between all three (Johnston 1997: 464). *Pay* is generally not distinguished from BEAT, although *way* may have a diphthong similar to that found in Mid-Northern.

2.2.3.5.2 *Insular Scots*

Figure 2.23 BAIT in Insular Scots

BAIT	
Shetland	Generally merger with MATE-HAME and BEAT Many DRESS words are also associated with this merger
Orkney	Generally merger with MATE-HAME and BEAT Many DRESS words are also associated with this merger

In Insular Scots, BAIT is generally either nearly or fully merged with BET (although the vowel in BAIT may be longer and have an off-glide). Phonetically, this vowel can vary from a fairly high monophthong on the west of the mainland of Shetland, [eː], to diphthongs of a variety of different heights on the periphery of that archipelago, to a low front monophthong in parts of Orkney (before voiceless stops), so that *bait* is [bæːt].

In Orcadian and the dialects of northern Shetland MATE-HAME and BAIT generally merge in all environments. The same is true throughout both archipelagos before /r/, /s/ and velars, with the BAIT vowel normally standing for both, so that *taste* may sound like *test* to non-locals. Regularly, *rain*, and, rather less regularly, *tail*, take a glide vowel before the final consonant. *Pay* and *way* have [εɪ] throughout the dialect area (ibid.: 464). Outsiders at least may hear this vowel as a variant of BITE.

2.2.3.6 DRESS

As Johnson (1997: 470) points out, the Scottish realisation of /ε/ 'may be slightly more peripheral or higher than a typical English or American BET form'. When speaking SSE, Scottish speakers generally have the same distribution patterns as any other variety of Standard English. When speaking Scots, however, in anything other than the 'thinnest' possible variety, a number of words associated with other sets may have this vowel. Examples of this include the Scots equivalents to *grass* and *after*, regularly /grεs/ and /ˈεftər/, although the former is often *girse* /gɪrs/ in our dialects. On the other hand, a number of words associated with DRESS in the Standard, such as *dead, head, red, well* (adverb) and *deaf*, are associated with the BEAT group (see above). Because DRESS vowels behave differently before /r/ in some of our dialects, I have distinguished a sub-set PERCH.

2.2.3.6.1 Northern Scots

Figure 2.24 DRESS in Northern Scots

DRESS	
MNA	Merged with MATE-HAME and BAIT
MNB	Distribution mainly as with SSE
NNA	Distribution mainly as with SSE
NNB	Distribution mainly as with SSE
SN	Distribution mainly as with SSE Southern Angus and Dundee: *bag*
PERCH	
MNA	Often *start, starve, farm, heart, arse*
MNB	Often *start, starve, farm, heart, arse*
NNA	Often *start, starve, farm, heart, arse* *mare* 'more', *mare* 'female horse' Sporadic merger with SKIRT and NURSE
NNB	Often merger with SKIRT and NURSE Often *start, starve, farm, heart, arse* *mare* 'more', *mare* 'female horse'
SN	Often *start, starve, farm, heart, arse* Southern Angus and Dundee: *bairn* 'child'

In Mid-Northern A, the DRESS vowel is generally raised and merged with MATE-HAME and BAIT at /e/, pronounced somewhat lower in the mouth than it is in central Scotland. I hear *glaikit*, 'simple, gormless', for instance, as if it had /ɛ/, in contrast with my own higher Central Scots pronunciation. To natives of the North-East, however, words of this type are associated with the merged /e/ vowel. In Mid-Northern B, North Northern and South Northern, this merger generally did not take place, and an /ɛ/ pronunciation is more normal for DRESS. This vowel is often raised somewhat and may even be diphthongised. This diphthongisation is often seen as typical of Moray speech, but is found as far south as Angus (Johnston 1997: 472). Monophthongal pronunciations are the norm in North Northern, however.

In Northern Scots, a preceding <wr> (generally /vr/), in words like *wretch* (local *vratch*), /w/, as in *well*, 'place where water is drawn' (local *wall*), and *web* (local *wab*), or a preceding palatal consonant and /l/

following, as in *shell* or *yellow*, normally leads to the vowel being transferred to TRAP, so that *yellow* is /ˈjalə/ and *shell* /ʃal/. *Web* may, in some communities, become associated with LOT (ibid.: 472), as /wɔb/. In coastal communities, diphthongisation may lead to *web* becoming associated with LOWP, as /wəub/. This last change forms part of *dog-diphthongisation*, and will be dealt with in the discussion of LOT.

2.2.3.6.2 Insular Scots

Figure 2.25 DRESS in Insular Scots

DRESS	
Shetland	Some merger with BAIT, MATE-HAME, BEAT
Orkney	Some merger with BAIT, MATE-HAME, BEAT
PERCH	
Shetland	Often *start, starve, farm, heart, arse* *war, far, warn*
Orkney	Often *start, starve, farm, heart, arse* *war, far, warn*

In Insular Scots, as well as the general Scots exceptions detailed above, a number of further special developments are present for the equivalent to Standard DRESS. Particularly in Shetland, vowel lengthening is possible before /k/ (ibid.: 471), so that *peck* may well be [peːk] or [pɛːk]. This vowel is often pronounced in these dialects in a similar (if not identical) way to the reflexes of BEAT and MATE-HAME and BAIT. Before voiced sounds [ɛ] can rise almost, or completely, to [e]. Although found throughout both archipelagos, this development is, again, particularly strong in Shetland. In central and southern Shetland, an up-gliding diphthong pronounced [ɛɪ] or [eɪ] may be heard in words like *beg*. In the outer isles, such as Whalsay, a more centralised diphthong, [ɜi], is found, sounding, at least to outsiders, almost identical to BITE.

As in SSE, *egg* is generally pronounced with DRESS in Shetland. The word is pronounced with /i/ in the conservative Fair Isle dialect (ibid.: 471), thereby transferring to MEET. This pronunciation was probably more common in the past.

Orcadian is more like Northern Scots than is Shetlandic. This can be seen in particular with the development of /ɛ/ following /w/, in words such as *web* or *well*, which merge with TRAP. Like Shetland, however, but in a much more circumscribed way, /ɛ/ can be raised, on this occasion before /l/ to [e] in the Kirkwall area (so that *bell*, *bail*, and *bale* may become homophones) or [ɜ] in North Ronaldsay. This phenomenon is not found elsewhere in the islands, however.

2.2.3.7 TRAP

Because of the presence in all the varieties under discussion of pre-consonantal and word-final /r/ and the lack of a phonemically qualitative distinction (as found in RP) between the vowels in *trap* and *bath*, Wells' TRAP, BATH, PALM and START lexical sets are one set in most forms of SSE and in all Scots varieties. Phonemically, the vowel in question is /a/, although there can be considerable variation from place to place over pronunciation, in frontness or backness, or vowel height (Johnston 1997: 484).

A number of words which belong to this set in SSE are associated with other sets in most of the Scots dialects. Words such as *arm*, often *part*, *airt*, 'place', and *bairn*, 'child', are associated with MATE-HAME; other words, such as *start*, *starve*, *farm* and *arse* are often pronounced as DRESS; in Insular varieties, words such as *war*, *far* and *warn* also merge with DRESS.

In many Scots dialects, *hand-darkening* (ibid.: 484) takes place. Words with /r/, /rC/ (where *C* stands for any consonant), /l/ and /nd/, such as *tar*, *dark*, *pal* and *hand* merge with THOUGHT, realised according to the phonemic pattern of the variety concerned.

2.2.3.7.1 *Northern Scots*

Figure 2.26 TRAP in Northern Scots

TRAP	
MNA	*Wash, water, long, strong, top, off, loft* Some merger or overlap with CAUGHT Some palatalisation before or after velars: /ja/ in *bake, cake*
MNB	*Wash, water, long, strong, top, off, loft* Some merger or overlap with CAUGHT Some palatalisation before or after velars: /ja/ in *bake, cake*
NNA	*Wash, water, top, off, loft* *Long* and *strong* are not members of TRAP for all speakers Some merger or overlap with CAUGHT
NNB	*Wash, water, long, strong, top, off, loft* Some merger or overlap with CAUGHT
SN	*Wash, water, long, strong, top, off, loft* Some merger or overlap with CAUGHT

A number of words belonging to other sets in SSE are found with TRAP in most Scots dialects. These are often preceded by /w/, such as *wash* and *want*, or followed by /n/, such as *long*, /laŋ/, or *strong*, /straŋ/ (or in Scots *thrang*, 'crowded, extremely busy') (Johnston 1997: 484). *Top, off, loft* and *croft* as well as the diminutives *Rab* (*Robert*) and *Tam* (*Thomas*) also merge with TRAP. Some speakers would include the first syllable in *Forfar* in this set, as /ˈfarfər/.

Many Northern Scots varieties show a merger, or at least overlap, with THOUGHT, so that *caught* may be a homophone of *cat*, both being pronounced /kat/. This merger is confined to fewer and fewer environments the farther away from the Mid-Northern A area you go (ibid.: 485). Even within Mid-Northern A, the merger is more complete in the urban varieties of Aberdeen than in the rural varieties. With the exception of the north coast of Caithness, most varieties have at least overlap between the two classes before voiceless fricatives and many velars, so that *tack* and *talk*, may sound very similar, and might actually be homophones for native speakers: /tak/. This merger may still be spreading in North Northern, since it is associated primarily with the Thurso and Wick dialects, and with the speech of the fishing community, which, as we have seen, appears to be innovative in this area.

The place of articulation for TRAP ranges from front to central realisations in Caithness dialects [a~æ] to much more back realisations in Mid-Northern of the [ɑ] type, a stereotypical feature of Northern speech to outsiders. This back variant is also present in Caithness after labials and before /l/, /n/ and /r/, so that the vowel in *bag* and *band* are pronounced with different allophones which, to outsiders, seem phonemes. [ɑ], particularly in its long variants, is also found before /l/, /n/, /x/ and /nd/ (except, again, on the north coast), as well as after labials in North Northern A. In these latter communities, the *long* words may be included with LOT (perhaps under the influence of SSE), so that *lack* and *long* will have different vowels.

In general, Mid-Northern speakers have back pronunciations for this set, with some variation in length and some fronting in fishing communities. In Mid-Northern A at least, there is a tendency for certain words, such as *bank*, *want* and *Grampian* to have a vowel similar to [ʌ] rather than [ɑ]. Whereas most Scots speakers would pronounce a difference between English *water*, /ˈwɔtər/, and Scots *watter*, /ˈwatər/, this may not be as distinctive for speakers of Mid-Northern, since both /ɔ/ and /a/ often fall together at /ʌ/: /ˈwʌtər/.

In some parts of Angus, most notably the suburbs of Dundee north to Arbroath, a very distinctive /ɛ/ pronunciation is found in these contexts before /b/ and /g/, so that *bag*, for instance, belongs in the DRESS set.

In all Northern Scots varieties, words such as *bairn* and *start* have left this class and merged with the MATE-HAME class. This is with the exception of Angus, where a lower /ɛr/ pronunciation, similar to that in Mid-Scots, is present, merging with DRESS.

In Mid-Northern at least, a number of words, such as *tyaave*, 'to struggle', and *myaave*, 'seagull', are pronounced with the TRAP vowel, preceded by /j/. In Mid-Scots, this set would be associated with a rounded CAUGHT pronunciation and not have the preceding semi-vowel or succeeding /v/.

2.2.3.7.3 *Insular Scots*

Figure 2.27 TRAP in Insular Scots

TRAP	
Shetland	*Wash, water, long, strong, top, off, loft* Some merger or overlap with CAUGHT
Orkney	*Wash, water, long, strong, top, off, loft* Some merger or overlap with CAUGHT

In general, Insular Scots varieties realise a fronted [a] for this set, which is often somewhat higher in the mouth than the cardinal vowel, approaching /æ/. Many of the words associated with TRAP in Northern Scots are also included in this set in Insular Scots. Before /p/ and /k/ the vowel is always lengthened in Fair Isle and on the northern and southern periphery of the Orkneys, so that *cap* is [kaːp] and *back* is [baːk]. This implies, in these locations, a merger with CAUGHT, or even, with the fronted allophones found on Fair Isle, DRESS. Lengthening is also a feature of many dialects (although more common on the periphery of the archipelagos) before /b/ and /d/, producing realisations such as [kɛːb] for *cab* and [bɛːd] in Fair Isle and elsewhere, again merging with DRESS. The extent of lengthening and raising is a marker of local identity, even within relatively circumscribed areas, as can be seen in the western Shetland recording transcribed in 7.1.6 (pp. 156–61).

This lengthening is extended to environments before /g/ in a number of places around the archipelagos, so that *leg* is [laːg]. In North Ronaldsay, however, the vowel is backed to [ɔ] before /b/ and /d/, so that *lad* is [lɔd]. This causes overlap, if not merger, with LOT and GOAT. A following /g/ produces the expected [ɛː]. Natives of Yell are noted for pronouncing *tattie*, 'potato', as *tottie*. *Hand-darkening* also occurs in these varieties, generally producing a vowel like [ɑ] in words like *land* – [lɑnd], thus merging with CAUGHT.

2.2.3.8 KIT

In SSE the vowel /ɪ/ is generally employed in the same places as it is in RP, with the proviso that it is also realised as /ɪr/ with words such as *bird* in many accents, in distinction to the vowel in words such as *herd* and *fur*, with which it is merged in many varieties of English. Because of the variation in pronunciation with this set in these contexts, a sub-class, SKIRT, is also recognised. It is generally pronounced 'a good deal lower' in the mouth in most Scottish accents than it would be in RP (Johnston 1997: 468). This means that caricatures of Scottish speech often have a full merger between KIT and STRUT (Wells 1982: 2.2.5); this is not regularly the case for most speakers, however.

2.2.3.8.1 Northern Scots

Figure 2.28 KIT in Northern Scots

KIT	
MNA	*hit, grin, flit,* 'move house', *hill, pill* *foot* *speak, week, breeks* 'trousers'
MNB	*hit, grin, flit, hill, pill* *foot* *speak, week, breeks* 'trousers'
NNA	*hit, grin, flit, wind, hill, pill* *foot*
NNB	*hit, grin, flit, lid, bin, wind, hill, pill* *foot*
SN	*hit, grin, flit* *foot* *speak, week, breeks* 'trousers'
SKIRT	
MNA	Distribution mainly as with SSE
MNB	Distribution mainly as with SSE
NNA	Distribution mainly as with SSE Nairn: merger with NURSE
NNB	Merger with NURSE and PERCH
SN	Distribution mainly as with SSE

In Mid-Northern Scots, /ɪ/ is normal in these contexts. Words like *king*, however, can be pronounced with /i/, thus merging with MEET. *Kick* is not involved in this merger. *Wind* is generally merged with STRUT, although, unlike Central Scots, this does not happen with *hill* or *pill*. *Speak*, *week* and *breeks*, 'trousers', are all pronounced with the KIT vowel by traditional dialect speakers.

In North Northern A (in particular the Black Isle), KIT merges with STRUT before /d/ and /n/, although this is not carried out systematically. Thus *lid* and the first syllable in *Luddite* could be pronounced in the same way, as could *bin* and *bun*. In Nairn, /ɪ/ before /r/ is merged with NURSE, so that *girl* has the same vowel as *fur*, a sub-set of STRUT in most Scottish accents. This merger has not happened on the Black Isle. *Swim* and *king* (on this occasion including *kick*) are pronounced /i/ and are merged with FLEECE. *Night* (pronounced /nɪxt/) is not involved in this merger. *Hill*, *pill* and *wind* are pronounced with [ɪ], however.

In Caithness the subsets *swim* and *king* are pronounced /i/, although native speakers report that the words which have /i/ or /ɪ/ can vary at a very local level indeed. Wick is /wik/ for traditional speakers. As we will also see for Insular Scots, a following /x/ causes a diphthong to be pronounced in place of the /ɪ/, so that *night* can be /nəixt/ or /naext/. There is merger between SKIRT and NURSE; in recent times, as Johnston (1997: 469) points out, this combination has also merged with PERCH words (pronounced with a distinct /ɛr/ in most other Scottish varieties), so that Caithness speech is, in this context, rather like many Irish and North American English varieties.

South Northern varieties do not generally have the fronted /i/ pronunciations for the *swim* and *king* sub-classes. They do, however, have the retraction of /ɪ/ to /ʌ/ in words such as *hill*, *pill* and *wind*, characteristic of more central varieties. Again, this may represent in part the influence of Dundonian. These sub-classes are therefore transferred to STRUT. On the other hand, as with Mid-Northern, *speak*, *week* and *breeks*, 'trousers', are all pronounced with /ɪ/.

2.2.3.8.2 Insular Scots

Orcadian varieties generally have a more fronted realisation for /ɪ/ than is normal on the Scottish mainland, so that words like *hid* may be homonyms or near-homonyms of words like *heed*. Shetland varieties tend to be more retracted, however. This is particularly marked for the latter when /ɪ/ stands before labials and velars, so that, to outsiders at least, *nib* may sound like *nub*, *rig* like *rug*, and so on (although the normal Shetland pronunciation of STRUT means that there is little danger of confusion).

Figure 2.29 KIT in Insular Scots

KIT	
Shetland	*hit, grin, flit, lid, bin, wind, hill, pill* *foot* *speak*
Orkney	*hit, grin, flit, lid, bin, wind, hill, pill* *foot* Stronsay: merger with BUIT, except before /r/ or finally
SKIRT	
Shetland	Distribution mainly as with SSE
Orkney	Distribution mainly as with SSE

As with the mainland Northern varieties, Orcadian demonstrates a fronting of /ɪ/ in words like *swim*, *king*, and often *kick*, to /i/. In marked contrast to Mid-Scots varieties, where retraction to /ʌ/ is common, the vowel in *pill* and *hill* is often pronounced further forward in the mouth, as [ɛ]. To outsiders this sounds strikingly like DRESS, although it is doubtful whether it is anything more than an allophone of KIT to native speakers. In both insular varieties, a following /x/ may cause diphthongisation, so that *night* may be /nəixt/ or /naext/.

As was noted in 2.2.3.2 (pp. 29–31), a few words where SSE has /i/ before /k/, such as *week*, *breeks*, 'trousers', or *speak*, have /ɪ/ in at least some of our dialects, especially in Shetland.

2.2.3.9 STRUT
As with DRESS and KIT, some of our varieties distinguish between STRUT before /r/ and all other contexts. For this reason, a sub-set, NURSE, has been created.

2.2.3.9.1 *Northern Scots*
In all dialects of Northern Scots the STRUT vowel is generally pronounced /ʌ/. As has already been noted, the more central and lower pronunciation of KIT means that some outsiders may hear a merger between these sets. Although this does happen on occasion (see 2.2.3.8, p. 000 for details), they are generally kept separate in most varieties in most positions. A number of words pronounced with /u/ in Scottish Standard English, such as *bull* or *full*, may be pronounced with the STRUT vowel by some Scots speakers.

Figure 2.30 STRUT in Northern Scots

STRUT	
MNA	*cup, muck, bun, wind, dog* *want*
MNB	*cup, muck, bun, wind*
NNA	*cup, muck, bun* *lid, bin*
NNB	*cup, muck, bun*
SN	*cup, muck, bun, wind, dog* *hill, pill*
NURSE	
MNA	Distribution mainly as with SSE
MNB	Distribution mainly as with SSE
NNA	Distribution mainly as with SSE Nairn: merger with NURSE
NNB	Merger with SKIRT and PERCH
SN	Distribution mainly as with SSE

A number of words which are members of TRAP in many Scots dialects, such as *wash* and *watter*, 'water', are members of STRUT in Mid-Northern A. A number of COT words, such as *bother*, are also often pronounced with STRUT in that area (/ˈbʌðər/), even in SSE pronunciation. This may be an extension of the transfer found in many Scots dialects of words like *dog* to STRUT. This last change does not occur in North Northern or Mid-Northern B varieties.

With the NURSE sub-set, there is merger with the SKIRT sub-set of KIT in the Nairn area and with this sub-set and the PERCH sub-set of DRESS in Caithness. This is a feature which, along with other pronunciations discussed below, may make speakers of these dialects sound Irish to outsiders. These mergers are also occasionally heard in the pronunciation of middle-class speakers in Aberdeen; on this occasion, this is probably an importation from Edinburgh speech, however.

2.2.3.9.2 Insular Scots

In Insular Scots – particularly in Shetland varieties – some lip rounding may be heard in the pronunciation of words in this set. This can make islanders sound northern English to other speakers of Scots. *Dog* is not

Figure 2.31 STRUT in Insular Scots

STRUT	
Shetland	*cup, muck, bun* Distribution mainly as with SSE
Orkney	*cup, muck, bun* Distribution mainly as with SSE
NURSE	
Shetland	Distribution mainly as with SSE
Orkney	Distribution mainly as with SSE

a member of this set in the speech of most people from both archipelagos. Words in the NURSE sub-class are normally distinguished from words in the SKIRT sub-class.

2.2.3.10 OOT

2.2.3.10.1 Northern Scots

Figure 2.32 OOT in Northern Scots

OOT	
MNA	*mouth, mouse, louse, court, course, coarse* /j-/: *duck, tough* vestigial /j-/: *hook, poor*
MNB	*mouth, mouse, louse, court, course, coarse* /j-/: *duck, tough* vestigial /j-/: *hook, poor*
NNA	*mouth, mouse, louse, court, course, coarse* /j-/: *duck, tough, hook, poor*
NNB	*mouth, mouse, louse, court, course, coarse* /j-/: *duck, tough, hook, poor*
SN	*mouth, mouse, louse, court, course, coarse* /j-/: *duck, tough* vestigial /j-/: *hook, poor*

As we have noted before, a considerable number of words, mainly spelled <ou> and pronounced with a diphthong in Standard English, forming part of Wells' MOUTH set, are pronounced with a monophthong /u/ in Scots. My own intuition is that this pronunciation is particularly typical of Scottish speech and therefore has survived better than many other sets, native speakers often seeing the pronunciations, for instance, /mus/ and /məus/, 'mouse', as cognate forms ('Scots' and 'English') rather than variants. A number of words, such as the equivalents of *court* and *course*, are pronounced with /o/ in SSE, but /u/ in Scots. The same is true for *coarse*.

There is considerable variation in the Scots dialects over the level of fronting found with this vowel. Johnston (1997: 475) presents a pattern whereby central to front variants [y~ ʉ~ Y] are associated with, on the one hand, Caithness, and on the other South Northern. He suggests that the former is a development independent from the latter, which is part of an ongoing fronting spreading from the Central Belt. But at the start of the twenty-first century (some thirty years after the recordings Johnston uses), the fronted pronunciations are heard throughout the North-East with the exception of middle-aged and older Mid-Northern B speakers and some older people in certain contexts in Mid-Northern A.

In some Mid-Northern areas, diphthongisation takes place with a few members of this set. I am most aware of this with older speakers serving in shops, who may introduce a transaction with [nəu], 'now'. This appears to be triggered by the context, since the same speakers would generally use /nu/ in other contexts.

A sub-set of OOT are the NEW words, which, again, take front or back reflexes depending on provenance. In general, younger speakers of Mid-Northern A have fronted pronunciations for these words, although I have heard more back pronunciations with younger speakers with the equivalent to English *duck*, pronounced /djuk/ or even /dʒuk/. The cognate of English *tough*, *teuch*, is pronounced /tjux/ or /tʃux/, again, often with a more back /u/ than is usually present in other contexts. Conversely, the Aberdeenshire village *Tough* is /tux/.

A number of words with /ju/ in Standard English, such as *few*, are members of LOWP in some areas; others, such as *use*, are historically members of BUIT. In the North-East, for instance, *few* is often /fjəu/ and *use* (noun) /is/.

2.2.3.10.2 Insular Scots

In Insular varieties, back allophones are much more common than front for OOT, although, as elsewhere in Scotland, the latter are becoming increasingly common, particularly in Orkney. /ju/ is still found with words like *duck* and *tough*. In Orkney in particular, many BUIT words are pronounced with /u/, especially before /r/. This may be a borrowing from the SSE system. Many members of LOWP – including *lowp*, 'leap', itself – are often transferred to this set by insular speakers.

Figure 2.33 OOT in Insular Scots

OOT	
Shetland	*mouth, mouse, louse, court, course, coarse* *lowp* 'leap', *rowie* 'bread roll' /j-/: *duck, tough*
Orkney	*mouth, mouse, louse, court, course, coarse* Often, BUIT before /r/ (*poor*, etc.) /j-/: *duck, tough*

2.2.3.11 GOAT

In SSE, many words are associated with this set, generally pronounced /o/. The primary spellings for this set are <o, oCe, oa>, with a sub-set of <ol, ow> spellings. As has been noted, many words which are represented by <oa> spellings in particular are members of MATE-HAME in Northern and Insular Scots, while many <ow> and <ol> words are associated with LOWP. That does not mean that /o/ is entirely unknown, however. Indeed, a number of highly distinctive Scots words, such as *gloaming*, 'twilight', contain the sound.

2.2.3.11.1 Northern Scots

Figure 2.34 GOAT in Northern Scots

GOAT	
MNA	General move towards merger with CAUGHT; partial merger with COT /j-/: *poke* 'bag'; *boke* 'vomit'
MNB	General move towards merger with CAUGHT; partial merger with COT /j-/: *poke* 'bag'; *boke* 'vomit'
NNA	General move towards merger with CAUGHT
NNB	General move towards merger with CAUGHT
SN	General move towards merger with CAUGHT; partial merger with COT

In Northern Scots, GOAT, pronounced with /o/ in SSE, and CAUGHT, pronounced as /ɔ/ in SSE, may merge, although, with a few exceptions, this merger is partial and constrained by the environment. This merger can be at a higher /o/ position, or at a lower /ɔ/, again depending upon environment. The merger seems to be most complete in Aberdeen and its immediate hinterland. It is particularly strong in contexts where /r/ follows, especially where there is a further following consonant. Thus *force* may have a lowered vowel, while *bore* may not (ibid.: 480). This distinction is unusual in most Central Scots pronunciations.

In most parts of northern Scotland the vowel is back and monophthongal, although mid or front forms are spreading in South Northern, and diphthongal pronunciations may be found in areas close to the Highland line, such as Nairn and the Black Isle. Diphthongal realisations are also common (as throughout Scots) before /d/ in words like *road*. A similar diphthongal pronunciation is also regularly found before /n/, as in *phone*, and /r/, as in *roar*. Native speakers appear to consider these differences to be phonetic rather than phonemic.

This is in marked contrast to the treatment of GOAT before /b/, in words like *robe*, and /g/, in words like *rogue*, as well as with single words, such as *hope*, pronounced /həup/ in Caithness, on the north coast of Mid-Northern A (and Moray to some extent also), representing an extension of the diphthongisation of CAUGHT before /g/ in words like *dog* in these areas (ibid: 480). These items are therefore transferred to LOWP.

Coat and *coal* are transferred to BITE in traditional Mid-Northern A. We will discuss this further with BITE.

After /p/ and /b/, there is often a /j/ glide before GOAT in Mid-Northern, leading to pronunciations such as /pjok/ for *poke*, 'bag', and /bjok/ for *boke*, 'vomit'. The second element is particularly low here, often leading to transfer to CAUGHT.

2.2.3.11.2 *Insular Scots*

Figure 2.35 GOAT in Insular Scots

GOAT	
Shetland	General move towards merger with CAUGHT Southern Shetland: merged with COT and CAUGHT
Orkney	General move towards merger with CAUGHT

In Insular Scots, COT and GOAT are almost completely merged, except in a number of contexts in Orcadian in particular, especially before /r/, as with *ford*, /ford/, in distinction to *cord*, /kɔrd/. When they are distinguished, this appears to be largely due to borrowing from SSE. GOAT can be pronounced with a diphthong in the islands, although this is not as widespread as it is in northern Scotland (ibid.: 479).

2.2.3.12 CAUGHT

In most forms of SSE, CAUGHT and COT (including their rhotic sub-sets) are, unlike most varieties of English, merged, in a vowel /ɔ/. This pattern is also normal for most Central and Southern Scots dialects, although the actual realisation for both may often be closer to /o/. Northern and Insular dialects maintain at the very least vestiges of the original split between the two sets, however. Because of this they will be treated as separate, but inter-related, sets.

As well as the expected CAUGHT words, most Scots dialects would include the Scots reflex of *old* as well as those contexts where /l/ has been 'lost', such as *all* (Scots *aw*) or *fall* (Scots *faw*) within this set.

2.2.3.12.1 *Northern Scots*

Figure 2.36 CAUGHT in Northern Scots

CAUGHT	
MNA	Near-merger with COT; move towards merger with GOAT; move towards merger with TRAP
MNB	Near-merger with COT; move towards merger with TRAP
NNA	Near-merger with COT; move towards merger with TRAP
NNB	Near-merger with COT; move towards merger with TRAP
SN	Merger or near-merger with COT; move towards merger with GOAT

In Mid-Northern, North Northern A and South Northern dialects there is a general tendency for CAUGHT to approach, or achieve, merger with TRAP, the difference between the two often being a matter of vowel length. Thus *cat*, *caa't* ('call it') and *caught* are at least near-homophones. In Angus, however, Mid-Scots /ɔ/ is increasingly present in these contexts, probably under the influence of Dundonian speech. The local pronunciations of *half* and *old* form part of this set.

In Caithness, CAUGHT is generally separate from TRAP, with a front pronunciation along the lines of long /a/. An exception to this is *half*, which is transferred to TRAP. The local reflex of *old* is generally diphthongal, merging with LOUP. It shares this feature with a number of Northern Isles dialects.

2.2.3.12.2 *Insular Scots*

In general, Insular Scots maintains a distinction between COT and CAUGHT, and between the latter and TRAP. The actual allophone

Figure 2.37 CAUGHT in Insular Scots

CAUGHT	
Shetland	Near-merger with COT and GOAT; move towards merger with TRAP Southern Shetland: merged with COT and GOAT; move towards merger with TRAP
Orkney	Near-merger with COT and GOAT; move towards merger with TRAP

employed can be associated with a variety of pronunciations, front or back, low or high, perhaps the most strikingly different of which being the [ɛː] found in North Ronaldsay and the [ɒː] of southern Shetland (Johnston 1997: 489). In the latter area CAUGHT normally merges with COT and GOAT, so that *tot*, *taught* and *tote* are homophones. STRUT, COT, CAUGHT and GOAT merge before /x/.

Old words can have the CAUGHT vowel throughout the archipelagos, although the diphthong heard in Caithness is also present. Many speakers also use a diphthongal pronunciation with *thought* and *brought*, with, or particularly without, /x/, thus merging with LOWP. In fieldwork carried out on Yell in 2005, this feature was associated by natives of the south of the island with speakers from the north of the island, so that *loch*, 'expanse of water', was /ləux/.

2.2.3.13 COT
As mentioned for TRAP, the most common exception to the uniform reflex /ɔ/ or its equivalent in the varieties of Scots is where the vowel is unrounded before labials, causing merger with TRAP. Thus *top* may be a homophone of *tap*.

2.2.3.13.1 Northern Scots
In Northern Scots, the further a speaker's place of origin is from the Aberdeenshire centre, the more likely they are to distinguish COT, /ɔ/ in SSE and GOAT, /o/ in SSE. In northern areas of South Northern, this merger is generally complete, so that *tot* and *tote* would be considered homophones. In Mid-Northern A proper, this merger has not been entirely accomplished, with a distinction between COT and GOAT possible at least before /t/ and /k/. In this area, therefore, *Paul* and *pole* would be homophones, but *tot* and *tote* would be minimal pairs. This merger is much less common in Mid-Northern B, and is largely avoided in both southern forms of South Northern and North Northern, since

Figure 2.38 COT in Northern Scots

COT	
MNA	Partial merger with GOAT; near-merger with CAUGHT; move towards merger with TRAP
MNB	Near-merger with CAUGHT; move towards merger with TRAP
NNA	Near-merger with CAUGHT; move towards merger with TRAP
NNB	Near-merger with CAUGHT
SN	Merger or near-merger with CAUGHT; move towards merger with GOAT; move towards merger with TRAP

COT is pronounced significantly lower in the mouth than is the case in Mid-Northern A. Before /n/, however, SSE /ɔ/ is replaced by /o/ in some places in Moray and Caithness, so that the first syllables in *Donald* and *donor* are pronounced the same way.

On the other hand, there are occasions where the northern periphery of the region appears innovative. In the eastern and southern areas of Mid-Northern A (including the city of Aberdeen) and South Northern, the local varieties share a development with more southern dialects whereby a lexically conditioned change of vowel from /ɔ/ to /ʌ/ takes place with words such as *dog* /dʌg/ and *bonnet* /'bʌnət/. As we have already seen with STRUT, this common tendency is extender by some speakers which would not normally go through the change, such as *bother*. In Caithness, Mid-Northern B and the north-west areas of Aberdeenshire, the latter lexical item goes through the expected merger, but the vowel in *dog* is diphthongal and merged with LOWP.

In Caithness (as well as Orkney) the vowel in SSE *home* and *bone* appear to be merged with this class. These pronunciations are often considered dialectal by native speakers.

2.2.3.13.2 *Insular Scots*

In Insular Scots, merger between COT and GOAT is generally present before /l/ and /r/, so that *Paul* and *pole*, as well as *horse* and *hoarse*, are homophones, no matter their actual place of articulation. As Johnston (1997: 482) points out, the same merger can also be found 'in a few central and southern Shetlandic and central Orcadian varieties, before /n/', so that *on* and *own* are homophones. The merger is also carried through before all stops (with the exception, in Shetland varieties, of /g/), so that *lob* and *lobe*, for instance, could be homophones.

Figure 2.39 COT in Insular Scots

COT	
Shetland	Partial merger with GOAT; move towards merger with TRAP Southern Shetland: merged with CAUGHT and GOAT; move towards merger with TRAP
Orkney	Partial merger with GOAT; near merger with CAUGHT; move towards merger with TRAP Many LOWP words included in this set

Dog diphthongisation is occasionally found in north and central Shetland varieties, as well as in South Ronaldsay (one of the closest islands to Caithness, it might be noted, where this pronunciation is common), so that *dog* is /dɔug/. Elsewhere, the mainstream Scots development to /ʌ/ is found in western Shetland varieties, as /dʌg/, the apparently standard /ɔ/ in southern Shetland.

A number of COT words not generally transferred to TRAP in other of our varieties, such as *hobby* and *Norway*, are transferred there in some varieties of Shetlandic, as shown in 7.1.2 and 7.1.5 (pp. 150 and 155).

2.2.3.14 TRY
In most varieties of English, words with the spellings <iCe> or <yCe> generally have a diphthongal pronunciation. This is also true for Scottish accents. But due to the effects of the Scottish Vowel Length Rule, two diphthongs rather than one are generally realised in these contexts, depending, in the main, on environment. I will follow Johnston (1997) in creating two sub-sets: TRY (the long variant) and BITE (the short).

The variant /ae/ is generally found in long contexts according to the Scottish Vowel Length Rule, in words such as *tied* (in comparison with *tide*), *five* and *size*. Scots mainly has the same distribution as SSE, although *die*, *fly* and *lie* often belong to MEET in Scots. The first element in the diphthong may differ from place to place in terms of frontness, depending largely upon the pronunciation of TRAP.

2.2.3.14.1 Northern Scots
In Mid-Northern Scots, some words with following or preceding /r/, such as *fire*, *drive* or *byre*, 'cow house', are pronounced with the BITE vowel. This is particularly noticeable in pronunciations such as /'bəiər/ *byre* rather than Mid Scots /'baeər/. Caithness Scots (as well as most varieties of South Northern) have /ae/ for this sub-set, however, making them closer to the Scots mainstream.

Figure 2.40 TRY in Northern Scots

TRY	
MNA	*cry, buy, size* *way, pay*
MNB	*cry, buy, size* *way, pay*
NNA	*cry, buy, size five, drive, byre* For some speakers: *way, pay*
NNB	*cry, buy, size* For some speakers: *way, pay*
SN	*cry, buy, size* *five, drive, byre*

2.2.3.14.1 Insular Scots

Figure 2.41 TRY in Insular Scots

TRY	
Shetland	*cry, buy, size* *five, drive, byre* Not well distinguished from BITE
Orkney	*cry, buy, size* *five, drive, byre* Not well distinguished from BITE

In Insular Scots, TRY and BITE appear almost to be merged. This will be discussed more fully with BITE.

2.2.3.15 BITE

2.2.3.15.1 Northern Scots

Although this class remains fairly stable in Northern Scots, the actual pronunciation of the first element of this diphthong varies considerably from [ʌ] in older people's speech in Caithness to [ɛ] on the Black Isle. The sub-set with following /d/ may be most likely to have a variant pronunciation (Johnston 1997: 494), although this veers towards more back in Mid-Northern to more front (and spreading to other contexts) in Caithness. In the border areas between Angus and Kincardineshire, words such as *dyke* may be pronounced /dek/ or /dɛk/, merging with BEAT (ibid.: 494). This may represent a borrowing from southern Angus

Figure 2.42 BITE in Northern Scots

BITE	
MNA	*time, bride, guide* *boil, hoist, spoil, joiner, oil* *wyme* 'belly' *quine* 'girl'; *sweat* *clythes* 'clothes' *fire, five, byre* /w-/: *coat, coal*
MNB	*time, bride, guide, boil, hoist, spoil, joiner, oil* *wyme* 'belly' *quine* 'girl'; *sweat* *clythes* 'clothes' *fire, five, byre*
NNA	*time, bride, guide* For some speakers: *way, pay* *boil, hoist, spoil, joiner, oil* *wyme* 'belly'
NNB	*time, bride, guide* For some speakers: *way, pay* *boil, hoist, spoil, joiner, oil* *wyme* 'belly' For some speakers: merger or near-merger with CHOICE
SN	*time, bride, guide* *way, pay* *boil, hoist, spoil, joiner, oil* *wyme* 'belly'

dialects (in particular Dundonian), where words associated with TRY and BITE are regularly pronounced /ɛ/, such as /pɛ/ for *pie*. This variant pronunciation has been borrowed into Mid-Northern A for at least one word. In Aberdeen a *Forfar bridie*, a pastry filled with minced meat and onions, is called a /'bredi/ or /'brɛdi/. In northern Buchan, however, this pastry is called a /'bradi/.

In Mid-Northern A varieties, /w/ is often found before GOAT when preceded by /k/, with fronting of the vowel, in words such as *coat*, pronounced /kwəit/, and *coal*, pronounced /kwəil/, with succeeding mergers. This may be an extension of similar developments with /g/ before BUIT, as with /gwid/ for *good*. This pronunciation is becoming rare even in rural areas.

The Caithness reflex of BITE approaches, if not actually merges with, the local reflex of CHOICE. This is a further feature of this dialect which makes outsiders sometimes confuse people from Caithness with people from Ireland.

2.2.3.15.2 Insular Scots

Figure 2.43 BITE in Insular Scots

BITE	
Shetland	*time, bride, guide* *way, pay* *boil, hoist, spoil, joiner, oil* Not well distinguished from TRY
Orkney	*time, bride, guide* *way, pay* *boil, hoist, spoil, joiner, oil* Not well distinguished from TRY

As has already been mentioned, the distinction between TRY and BITE is less clear-cut in Insular Scots than it is anywhere else. In Shetland, there is at least a phonetic distinction between two variant pronunciations in these contexts, based largely upon the level of fronting of the first element. Nevertheless, TRY pronunciations regularly appear in short environments where BITE would be absolutely demanded in Central Scots. In Orkney there is even less distinctiveness, with the *wide* sub-class regularly taking TRY vowels. The mainstream Scots distinction between *side* and *sighed* is not possible there. Ironically, this lack of distinction can make Insular speakers sound 'English' to mainland speakers. This lack of distinction can be seen as a more pronounced form of the use of TRY in words such as *way*, common in all Northern Scots dialects.

As with some South Northern varieties, Shetland varieties often have a monophthongal pronunciation in words like *dyke*, as [dek] or [dɛk]. Orcadian, however, does not have this development (Johnston 1997: 494).

2.2.3.16 LOWP, 'leap'

As was stated above, most of Wells' MOUTH set have a monophthongal pronunciation in Scots. The diphthong /əu/ is represented by a range of words in Scots not normally associated with it in Scottish Standard English, however.

2.2.3.16.1 Northern Scots

Figure 2.44 LOWP in Northern Scots

LOWP	
MNA	*lowp, rowie* 'roll', *bowl* 'kitchen depository' North coast: *hope*
MNB	*lowp, rowie* 'roll', *bowl* 'kitchen depository' *dog* North coast: *hope*
NNA	*lowp, rowie* 'roll', *bowl* 'kitchen depository' *old* *dog*
NNB	*lowp, rowie* 'roll', *bowl* 'kitchen depository' *dog*
SN	*lowp, rowie* 'roll', *bowl* 'kitchen depository'

A range of words with spelling <ow>, such as *grow* or <ol>, *roll*, generally treated as part of GOAT in SSE, are part of a diphthongal LOWP set in Scots (which also includes SSE pronunciations of OOT), where they are joined by specifically Scots words such as *knowe*, 'rocky hillock', *nowt*, 'cattle', and *howf*, 'small place to shelter in; cubby hole'. In the case of the <ol> class, the diphthongal pronunciation is also associated with the loss of /l/, as in Scots words such as *gowf*, 'golf' and *rowie*, 'bread roll, heavily interlarded with butter; an Aberdeen buttery'.

In Northern Scots there appears to be an ongoing change from 'back' pronunciations along the lines of [ʌu-ɒu] to more fronted ones, the most common being [əʉ]. Especially fronted pronunciations, such as [ɛʏ], are heard in Caithness. Johnson (1997: 498) associates the more back realisations with a large swathe of territory, including Mid-Northern A and B, the Black Isle and northern Angus, with it occurring 'even further south than that among older speakers'. His information is out of date, however. As we saw with OOT, back pronunciations can still be heard in the Mid-Northern Area (particularly in Mid-Northern B), especially from older speakers and even younger speakers from more traditional areas. The fronted allophones are taking over, however, even in Moray, as we can see in Mhairi Duncan's speech, analysed in 7.5 (p. 000) below.

The equivalent to English *through* is a member of this set in many parts of this region, being pronounced /θrəu/. A number of words which are spelt <ew> in English, most notably *few* and *dew*, form a sub-set of LOWP in Mid-Northern, being pronounced /fjəu/ and /djəu/ respectively. *Old* is often a member of this set in Caithness and the Northern Isles. Again, this can make Caithness speakers sound Irish.

2.2.3.16.2 *Insular Scots*

Figure 2.45 LOWP in Insular Scots

LOWP	
Shetland	*rowie* 'roll', *bowl* 'kitchen depository' Often, *dog*
Orkney	*rowie*, 'roll', *bowl*, 'kitchen depository' Often, *old* Often, *dog*

In Insular Scots, diphthongs along the lines of /əu/ are certainly present with this set, often with a rounded first element; fronted reflexes (as in Caithness) are prevalent on the peripheries of both archipelagos. Monophthongal variants are also possible, however, generally meaning that in Shetland many LOWP words are considered OOT words, including *lowp*, pronounced /lup/, and *ower*, 'over, very', pronounced /ur/. In Orkney, however, many LOWP words are considered COT words. *Howk*, 'pick at', is considered a member of COT on all occasions. *Thought* and *brought* often have LOWP pronunciations, however, as /θəuxt/ (or /θəut/) and /brəuxt/ (or /brəut/). Orcadians often pronounce *old* as /əuld/. *Dog* is often pronounced with this diphthong in both archipelagos.

2.2.3.17 CHOICE

Since most points on pronunciation and coverage of this lexical set are true for almost all of our dialects, the discussion of Northern and Insular features has been merged on this occasion.

In SSE almost all words spelled <oy> or <oi> are pronounced /ɔe/ (sometimes with a first element rather more like /o/). In Scots, however, the <oy~oi> words are generally split into two sets, one of which, JINE, is merged with sub-set of BITE. This sub-set includes the equivalents of *boil*, /bəil/, *joiner*, /dʒəinər/, *spoil*, /spəil/, and *oil*, /əil/. This distribution is fairly regular across northern Scotland and the Northern Isles, although borrowings from SSE are frequent even with the most common words and have entirely swamped the Scots variant in *coin*. Some Caithness speakers have transferred at least some members of BITE to this set; again, this may make the dialect sound 'Irish' to outsiders.

Figure 2.46 CHOICE in Northern and Insular Scots

CHOICE	
MNA	*boy, toy, ploy*
MNB	*boy, toy, ploy*
NNA	*boy, toy, ploy*
NNB	*boy, toy, ploy* For some speakers: merger or near-merger with BITE
SN	*boy, toy, ploy*
Shetland	*boy, toy, ploy*
Orkney	*boy, toy, ploy*

2.2.4 Discussion

At first glance, the vowel patterns of the Northern Scots dialects can appear deeply confusing and confused. Certainly, for a relatively small area, considerable variation is present: considerably more variation than can be found for the somewhat larger Mid-Scots area, in fact. The topography of the region, connected to the difficulties of long-distance travel through the area until very recently, possibly explains this variation. I would argue, however, that this apparent confusion masks a number of general tendencies.

In the first place, all of the Northern Scots dialects are, to a lesser or greater extent, deeply conservative in the vowel systems, their speakers regularly using pronunciations of particular words which are rarely, if ever, hear in Mid-Scots. The number of separate pronunciation sets is also somewhat larger for all of these dialects than is the case for more southern dialects. Nevertheless, a feature of all the dialects is merger between vowels which may be separate in SSE. None of the varieties ever realises all of the potential vowel contrasts.

There appear to be two areas within the region from which innovations are spreading: Mid-Northern (particularly Mid-Northern A) and Caithness. The latter is something of a surprise, given the low population of that county. It is worth bearing in mind, however, that this small population is still greater than are the Scots-speaking areas of the Black Isle and its hinterland.

We can distinguish to some extent between these two zones of innovation. Many of the features which are spreading from Mid-Northern A can be seen to encourage greater distinctiveness in local dialects in relation to the central dialects (although this is not true of the spread of fronted allophones of /u/); the innovations which are spreading from Caithness appear to be bringing the local dialects into line with more southern varieties, although it is unlikely that the southern varieties are acting upon Caithness dialect independently. These innovations have probably developed independently in the far north.

The Insular dialects are in many ways similar to the most conservative Northern varieties. Sometimes, in fact, their conservatism, in particular in the preservation of BUIT as a separate entity, is particularly striking. It is certainly true that more words are still associated with their native pronunciation (rather than their SSE association) in the islands than in Northern Scots or, indeed, another Scots variety. Both Orcadian and Shetlandic exhibit considerable variation within relatively circumscribed areas, something we would expect in island communities. Of the two, Shetlandic has preserved the most local pronunciation associations.

Finally, it has to be recognised that many of the most distinctive of local pronunciations co-exist with SSE variants. There is some evidence that, over time, the SSE pronunciations are gradually replacing the local variants.

2.3 Consonant phonology

In general, Northern and Insular Scots dialects have the same consonant patterns as all other varieties of Scots. They possess, for instance, a velar fricative /x/ with a palatal allophone [ç], the latter realised where there is significant fronting in either a preceding or following vowel. Dialects throughout the region have preserved /x/ in their traditional Scots distribution in words such as *nicht*, 'night', as well as in place names, as elsewhere in Scotland. In more traditional Mid-Northern areas, words with /xt/ in other Scots varieties, such as *micht*, 'might', and *dochter*, 'daughter', are pronounced with /θ/: *mith* and *dother*. This development (also found in more widespread distribution with *drouthie*, 'thirsty, desirous of strong drink', from *drought*) appears to be recessive; it is regularly represented in written North-East Scots, however.

Unusually for Scots, some areas, most notably the Black Isle and some fishing communities on the coasts of Mid-Northern A and B, can realise apparently /h/-free pronunciations along the lines of many traditional dialects of England. The origin of this process is obscure; the usage is highly recessive. Elsewhere, /h/ use mirrors that found throughout Scots, with /h/ being pronounced at all times except, occasionally, in unstressed contexts, particularly with personal pronouns.

The pronunciation of <wh> words varies considerably. In Mid-Northern A and Mid-Northern B, as well as in Caithness, <wh> was historically pronounced /f/ in all positions. As we will see in Chapter 5, there is an ongoing process of this sound being replaced by SSE /ʍ/ in all but interrogative and relative pronominal contexts. In South Northern, it is only in these latter contexts that the apparent change /ʍ/ > /f/ occurs at all. In traditional pronunciations on the Black Isle, no fricative is pronounced at all in <wh> position, so that Scots *whit*, 'what', is pronounced /ɪt/ ; this appears to be in line with the /h/ loss also recorded for this area. /f/ and /ʍ/ realisations are also used by local speakers, however.

/ʍ/ pronunciations are natural in the speech of younger inhabitants of even the heartland of Mid-Northern A; there is some evidence that this was not the case until very recently, however. Speakers of traditional rural North-East dialects above the age of seventy will, when speaking Standard English, often use a pronunciation [xʍ] for <wh>. This suggests a rather uncomfortable 'school' phoneme.

The combination /ŋg/ in words like English *finger* or *hunger* appears to be an introduction from SSE pronunciation, with /ŋ/ being the norm in dialect pronunciations.

In the Northern Isles, many speakers in Orkney and some in Shetland will conflate the pronunciation of /kw/ and /ʍ/ so that <qu> words are pronounced as if they were <wh>- Thus *queen* and *wheen*, 'a great many', may be homophones, pronounced /ʍin/. Conversely, many speakers from northern Shetland in particular would also conflate the two pronunciations, but pronounce them as /kw/. This development is in line with trends in the West Norse dialect continuum of which Shetland was until comparatively recently a part.

Many speakers in the Northern Isles – in particular residents of Whalsay – also have some degree of palatalisation between /g/ and especially /k/ and a front vowel, so that, for instance, *Kate* might be pronounced /kjet/ or even [çet]. Similar processes are also found in Mid-Northern A, in particular on the North Coast, so that, very typically, elderly traditional speakers may pronounce *gang*, 'to go', as /gjaŋ/ or even /dʒaŋ/.

Many insular and some mainland speakers pronounce initial /dʒ/ as /tʃ/. *John* is often /tʃɔn/, for instance. On the mainland this devoicing might be due to Gaelic influence. This is unlikely for the Northern Isles, however; particularly for Shetland. /tʃ/ is often /ʃ/ in Caithness, where Gaelic influence *is* likely.

In Shetland, traditional dialect speakers do not have /θ/ or /ð/ in initial or medial position, /t/ or /d/ being used instead; there are remnants of this in Orcadian dialects, although /θ/ is now found in initial contexts in words such as *thoo*, 'thou'. The latter is probably a borrowing from Scots, however, rather than a local development.

In North-East Scots, initial /ð/ is generally 'lost' in low-stress environments such as demonstrative or relative pronouns, so that the equivalent of *this* would be /ɪs/. A number of words with final /ðər/ in SSE, such as *father*, *mother*, *brother* and *other*, have /dər/ in North-East Scots; in particular in Buchan: *fadder*, *midder*, *bridder* and *idder*. The /r/ pronunciation for /ð/ found in some urban Mid-Scots pronunciations is not present anywhere in this region. As with other eastern Scots varieties, *though* is pronounced with initial /θ/.

In some Shetland varieties – most notably, but not uniquely, Whalsay dialect – *school* can be pronounced /styl/. Conversely, *lot* may on occasion be /lɔk/.

/l/ is generally back 'dark' [ɫ] throughout the region (although front /l/ is present in the Northern Isles). This is particularly noticeable along the former Gaelic linguistic frontier. As with other Scots varieties, /l/ has been 'lost' in syllable final position in the equivalents to *all, fall, wall*, and so on.

/r/ varies across the region. In Mid-Northern and South Northern, as well as the Northern Isles, a tap [ɾ] is most common. In some areas, most notably northern Angus and the Garioch, uvular [ʁ] pronunciations are sufficiently common to be considered more than personal idiosyncrasies or even defects, as elsewhere in Scotland. A retroflex [ɻ] is found in the North-East as well, but is the norm in North Northern, where it is probably a transfer from Gaelic. Final and medial /r/ loss in words like *car* and *cart* is beginning to spread from the Central Belt into South Northern and Aberdeen.

Glottalisation of /t/ is particularly common in the North-East (although it is heard in all dialects to some extent). Marshall (2003) argues that this is an urban feature being transferred from the Central Belt and beyond. It is worth noting, however, that, in my own experience, it is more common in rural speech – particularly when the speaker is from Buchan – than it is in Aberdeen City.

Because of its status as a relict and conservative area for Scots in particular and English in general, Northern and Insular Scots varieties maintain (or maintained until very recently) pronunciations no longer found elsewhere. The combinations <kn> and <gn> are particularly good examples of this. Both are sometimes pronounced as /kn/ in words like *knock*, 'clock', or /gn/ in *gnaw* in the Northern Isles. Until well into the twentieth century, this was also true for conservative rural Northern varieties, although only very elderly people are likely to pronounce them now. Nevertheless, the Moray equivalent for Shetland *knappin*, 'speaking in an affected or mincing manner; speaking in an Anglicised manner', is *gnyaapin*, with the /gn/ pronounced.

A distinction between <wr> and <r> in pronunciation is still present in Mid-Northern varieties. The historical initial /wr/ is realised as /vr/. Although in theory found with all <wr> words, it is particularly common nowadays with those words where there is another pronunciation distinction between Standard English and the local variety of Scots, such as *wretch* vs *vratch* /vratʃ/ or *wrong* vs *vrang* /vraŋ/, or where the English cognate is archaic, such as *vricht* /vrɪxt/, 'wright, carpenter'. The change from /wr/ to /vr/ may be a relict of a more general change from /w/ to /v/ in all contexts, which was later reversed.

2.4 Prosody

Very little work has been done on the prosody of these dialects, generally because their intonation patterns are very similar to those of more 'mainstream' Scots varieties, with the intonation rising on the first stress syllable of the clause.

The exception to this is Orcadian and (to some extent) Caithness speech, which has a highly characteristic 'singing' tone. So marked is this in Orkney speech that anecdotes abound of Orcadians being taken for Welsh people. Van Leyden (2004: 100) reports that the difference between Orcadian and Shetlandic prosody 'lies primarily in the alignment of the accent-lending pitch use. In Shetland this rise is located on the stressed syllable, while in Orkney it clearly shifts to the following, i.e. post-stress, syllable'. Reasons for this difference will be discussed in Chapter 5.

2.5 Conclusion

As this chapter demonstrates, the Scots dialects of northern Scotland and the Northern Isles exhibit considerable variation in pronunciation both between themselves and in relation to the patterns found for Central Scots. Yet this distinctiveness masks an underlying similarity: these dialects represent more conservative patterns which are associated with a greater range of words than would be the case in less traditional dialects.

3 Morphosyntax

3.1 Introduction

Unlike phonology and, in particular, lexis, morphosyntactic systems are quite stable and slow to change. Close relatives, such as Standard English and all of the Scots dialects, may not be as divergent in structure as they are in lexis and phonology. An absolute distinction between northern English and Scots usage rarely exists. Moreover, although elements of the grammar of the Northern and Insular dialects are sometimes different from other Scots varieties, most of what follows is true for all Scots dialects, unless otherwise stated. Finally, there have been generations of day-to-day contact with Standard English for all Scots speakers, both in writing and, latterly, in speech. There is much carry-over from one system to the other. Many elements of both standard and colloquial English grammar are found in even the 'densest' Scots.

Conversely, since grammar distinctions are both more deeply embedded in a native speaker's consciousness (in the sense that we appear to be much less aware of using particular constructions than we are of using particular sounds or words) and are also least likely to be abandoned in adulthood for other patterns, hearing and reading constructions which native speakers would consider Standard English, but which are actually peculiarly Scottish, is common. Aitken (1979) termed usages of this type 'covert Scotticisms'. These represent those occasions where speakers believe that the structures they are employing are Standard English but which can cause a degree of confusion – or at least surprise – for people outside Scotland.

Consequently, this discussion will deal largely with those features of Northern and Insular Scots grammar which are either generally Scots, but not colloquial English, or, in particular, are distinctive for our region. Interested readers should look towards Beal (1997), Miller (2003), Purves (2002) and, in particular, Macafee (1992–) for a more in-depth treatment of the issues at hand.

3.2 The nouns

3.2.1 Plural marking

Most Scots nouns are declined in similar ways to their English equivalents, so that the plural of Scots *kirk* is *kirks*, just as the plural of
English *church* is *churches*. A number of Scots nouns do not take the
'regular' -*(e)s* plural forms, however, instead marking plural by the addition of -*(e)n*. Thus the plural of *ee*, 'eye', is *een*, of *shoe* (also pronounced
/ʃe/ or /ʃy/), *shune* (pronounced /ʃin/ in the North-East, /ʃin/ or /ʃɪn/
in Caithness and /ʃyn/ in Shetland and Orkney and some Angus
dialects). *Cou*, 'cow', takes plural *kye* in traditional dialects. The analogical plural *cous* is spreading rapidly in the North-East and elsewhere. In
Shetland at least, the plural of *ox* is often *owsen*. This form was once much
more common on the Scottish mainland. Plurals in -*r* also exist, or
existed, until recently, in the traditional dialects, including *breer*, 'eye-
brows, eyelashes', and *caur* (also *kaur*, 'calves').

Galluses, 'braces for holding up trousers', is an example of a 'double
plural', where the first plural -*s* on *gallows* was reinterpreted as part of a
singular noun with a 'new' plural ending added.

Until recently, the plural of Shetland *bridder*, 'brother', was *breider*.
Again, this form was once widespread in Scots (and also finds an echo in
English *brethren*).

/f/ and /θ/ are not normally voiced in Scots before a plural ending,
so that the plural of *knife* may be *knifes*, of *path*, /paθs/. In both Scots and
SSE, the plural form of *house* (or *hoose*) normally does not have voicing
on the consonant before the ending either. The voiced pronunciations
are often used in 'careful' speech, however.

Zero plural marking is also present in traditional dialects with nouns
of measurement and quantity, such as *five mile* or *twenty pound*, and with
the names of large domestic animals: for example, *twa big stot*, 'two big
young bulls'.

3.2.2 Noun diminutives

Many nouns take a diminutive suffix, often -*ie*, as in *mannie*, '(elderly)
man viewed in an affectionate or humorous way' and occasionally -*ock*
(represented by -*ag* in Caithness), as in *kittag*, 'the kittiwake'. The first
suffix seems particularly productive in the North-East. The addition of
-*ie* can sometimes affect the meaning of the word. For instance, *wife*,
'woman', becomes 'woman of middle age or older', with the addition of
this suffix. -*ie* and -*ock* can be used in combination; thus *playockie*, 'toy'.

3.2.3 Shetland 'grammatical gender' marking

In Shetland dialect, a number of nouns can be referred to using sex-specific pronouns, so that *sun* can be referred to as *he*, while *kirk*, 'church', can be referred to as *shö*, 'she'. Whether this is a relict of the Old Norse grammatical gender system, or is an extension of the habit found among all English speakers to personify certain objects considered affectionately or used regularly, referring to them as *she*, is beyond our scope (Robertson and Graham 1952: 2).

3.3 Pronouns

3.3.1 Personal pronouns

3.3.1.1 First-person singular

In subject contexts, the usual form is *A*, /a/, although diphthongal forms similar to *I*, /ae/, are often used in stressed contexts. The object form is *me*. The possessive form when used as a determiner (equivalent to English *my*) can be *ma* in Northern Scots, although *me* is also found, particularly with elderly rural speakers. It is regular in the Northern Isles. The equivalent of the English pronominal possessive *mine* (as in, *this is mine*) is often *mines*.

3.3.1.2 First-person plural

Generally, the subject form is *we*; the object is represented, particularly in stressed positions, by *hiz* or *huz*. When expressing possession as a determiner, the forms *oor* and *wir* (*wur*) are used, the former generally in stressed contexts. The pronominal equivalent is *oors*.

3.3.1.3 Second-person singular

Few Scots dialects now distinguish between singular and plural by employing the inherited forms, equivalent to English *thou* and *you*. For centuries, the original singular form *thoo* has retreated north in Scotland, so that it is now only 'healthy' in the Northern Isles. Memories of its use are particularly strong in the fishing communities of the Black Isle, where the form *thee* was used in both subject and object contexts.

It is possible that the form was reinforced in the Northern Isles by the presence of a similar form in the now moribund Scandinavian dialects. In Orkney, subject contexts are traditionally represented by *thoo*, object and possessive contexts by *thee*. Discussions with native speakers in 2005 suggested that this feature was now confined largely to the northern islands of the archipelago. The same forms are found in Shetland, although with the expected use of /d/ as initial consonant. Unlike Orkney, *du* is used by all speakers of traditional dialect, no matter their age or place of origin. The 'respectful' form is identical to the plural form, *ye* or *you*.

According to Robertson and Graham (1952: 3), the familiar form is employed in Shetland 'a) when addressing a friend, b) when speaking to someone younger, c) when speaking to animals. It is not commonly used by children speaking to their parents or to older people'.

This last feature is now less common. As Melchers (1985: 93–4) reports, most schoolchildren questioned in Shetland who used *du* in any form (generally those who had most attachment to the islands) employed it in almost all circumstances except when speaking to a schoolteacher. This was the situation found in fieldwork interviews in autumn 2005. Interestingly, many native speakers used *du* to the researchers (although most asked if that was acceptable).

The 'English' nature of the school in such traditional dialect contexts might encourage the use of the more 'respectful' pronoun, although Melchers notes (ibid.: 94): 'Many children stated that *du* could be used to address *some* teachers, provided they were Shetlanders', which suggests that 'home' community membership sometimes counts for more than position.

3.3.1.4 Second-person plural
Both *ye* and *you* are found in subject and object contexts; the latter may be more common in stressed environments. The possessive determiner is *your*, although an unstressed *yer* and a stressed *yeer* also exist. The pronominal possessive form is *yours*.

As was noted above, the second-person plural form is generally used for the singular in northern Scotland; traditional speakers in the Northern Isles only use it in its original plural contexts or where formality demand its use. The analogical plural form *yous* or *yez* is heard occasionally in Aberdeen, but is frowned upon by speakers of traditional dialects and educational authorities alike.

3.3.1.5 Third-person singular
The Scots forms for this person are similar to those for SSE, with the exception of the equivalent to *she*, which is often represented (on the mainland) as *shae* and (in Shetland) as *shö*. In unstressed contexts, /h/ is regularly elided with pronouns. Conversely, /h/ is found in stressed contexts with *hit*, 'it', and *hiz*, 'us'. The use in Shetland of *he* or *shö* with reference to inanimate objects was discussed in 2.3 above. *He* can also be

used in that dialect in reference to the weather: *He's a cowld day* (Robertson and Graham 1952: 13).

Although *its* is found even in the most traditional dialects, many speakers prefer *o it*, often shortened to *o't* (Caithness, *o'd*), as in *At's a bonnie baby, at. Faas the midder o't?* A new stressed form *hees* /hiz/, 'his', is sometimes heard in Northern Scots.

3.3.1.6 Third-person plural
The paradigm for this person is generally the same as that of SSE, with the exception of *thaim*, the stressed equivalent of *them*. As with other nonstandard varieties, *them* is often used in contexts which makes it synonymous with *those*. This is particularly prevalent in the speech of the young.

The use of Shetland *dey* as equivalent to SSE existential *there* is discussed in 3.3.5 (p. 70).

3.3.2 Demonstrative pronouns and determiners

As with many non-standard varieties of English, Scots dialects generally recognise a three-part, rather than a two-part, spatial pattern with the demonstrative pronouns. This means that, whereas Standard English makes a distinction between *proximal* (nearby, either physically or notionally) *this* and *distal* (distant, either physically or notionally) *that*, many other dialects make a distinction between proximal, distal and *hyper-distal*, the last referring to beings or objects either notionally or physically at a distance greater than that associated with *that*. In Northern and Insular Scots, this concept is represented by both *yon* and *thon*, for instance, *Hit's nae een o that eens, hit's een o thon* 'it's not one of those ones, it's one of those'. The two forms appear to be used interchangeably.

Again, as with many other British dialects, the /t/ in *that one* and *that other* often crosses from the end of one word to the beginning of the other, with 'new' forms with *the*, such as (in the North-East) *the teen* and *the tither* (or *tidder*) being common. Although occasionally heard independently of each other (and very occasionally without *the*), these forms survive best in collocation, for instance, *de teen wis peerier as de tidder* 'the one was smaller than the other'.

Throughout northern Scotland and the Northern Isles, traditional dialects do not have a discrete plural of *this* and *that*, using the same form in both contexts, such as *This rooms arena as warrm as that rooms* 'these rooms aren't as warm as those rooms'.

These forms occur regularly in speech even when the remainder of the discourse is in SSE. They may have a Gaelic origin. Developments in this system will be discussed in Chapter 5.

3.3.3 Relative pronouns

Although <wh> forms are present as relative pronouns in all varieties of Northern and Insular Scots (in their various regional forms, dependent upon the realisation of <wh>), there is little doubt that *that* (often in its reduced *at* form) is much more common than in Standard English. As Macafee (1992–) puts it: 'Scottish speakers regularly use *that* for personal antecedents and in non-restrictive clauses as well as for non-personal antecedents and restrictive uses', for instance: *The folk that we bed wi last year has come tae see us* instead of 'The people whom we stayed with last year have come to see us'.

Although the equivalent to the possessive *whose* is present (it is, for instance, not uncommon in the North East to hear *faas*, as in *At's the loon faas midder's deid*, 'that's the boy whose mother's dead'), a form *that's*, expressing the same relationship, is much more common, as in *The loon that's midder's deid telt me is himsel*, 'the boy whose mother is dead told me this himself'.

As with Standard English, the relative pronoun can be 'deleted' (be expressed in a zero form) when it is not the subject of its subordinate clause, as in 'The man we saw yesterday was run over by a bus' instead of 'The man whom we saw yesterday was run over by a bus'.

Unlike Standard English, however, the relative pronoun can also be 'deleted' when it is acting as subject of the subordinate clause, for instance *The man bed doun wir street his flittit*, 'the man who lived down our street has moved house', in particular with an existential main clause, as in *There's the man bed doun wir street*, 'there's the man who lived down our street'.

3.3.4 Interrogative pronouns

The Scots interrogative pronouns are generally similar to their English equivalents, bearing in mind the phonological distinctions between the different varieties. In general, however, *what*, in its various pronunciations, is more common than in Standard English, generally being preferred to *which*. *How* (in the North-East and elsewhere, *foo*) is often used to inquire about the purpose of an act rather than its manner of execution. Subsidiary forms, such as *whitna*, 'what kind of', are also common, particularly in the usage of the older generations.

3.3.5 Existential there and its dialect equivalents

Existential *there*, as found in constructions such as 'there are a lot of problems with this answer' is a common feature of all the dialects under discussion. As with many other non-standard varieties, there is a growing tendency for singular *is* to be used even when referring to a plural entity, as with 'there is a lot of problems with this answer'.

In Shetland, however, *dey* (presumably the third-person plural pronoun) can be used existentially, particularly, although not exclusively, with the past tense (Robertson and Graham 1952: 13): *dey wir a lock o problems wi dis answer*.

3.4 The definite article

In general, our varieties follow the same patterns for the use of the definite article as Standard English. Along with most other Scottish varieties, *the* can be used in some additional contexts where it would not be normal in the Standard English of England (although they may regularly occur in SSE), however. As Beal (1997: 361–3) points out, these 'exceptions' fall into a number of categories, including time expressions (*the day*, *the morn*, *the nou*, and so on), when reference is made to institutions rather than specific examples of this institution (*the school*, *the university*, *the kirk*, and so on), games (*the fuitbaa*, 'football, soccer', *the bingo*), directions (*up the road*, *doun the stair[s]*) and generic expressions (*the holidays*). I am not convinced by her view that these last few categories are more likely to 'remain in lower-class speech', since they can be regularly heard from speakers from across the social spectrum in northern Scotland and the Northern Isles. *The* is also occasionally employed with the names of languages and varieties, such as *The Gaelic* or *The Doric*. Along with other non-standard varieties, certain idioms, such as *the wife* in place of *my wife*, are common. One informant from Yell used *the* when referring to her grandmother and grandfather. This might be interpreted as a mark of respect.

This usage is extended to other items 'possessed' by an individual, so that it is quite possible to hear someone say *A'll jist lea the handbag here*, 'I'll just leave my handbag here', when referring to one that is actually in that person's possession. Conversely, *your* (in its various forms) can be used generically where Standard English uses *the*, as in *Noo, tae that side ye'll see yer post office*, 'Now, to that side you'll see the post office'. Personal pronouns can also be found where no pronoun would be realised at all in Standard English, as in *At's me awaa til me bed*, 'I am about to go to bed'.

In the North East, *the*, in common with other determiners and pronouns, is regularly realised without initial /ð/, whether in stressed position (/i/) or unstressed (/ə/). The local name for the dialect, *the Doric*, is regularly /i ˈdɔrɪk/. A similar phenomenon is found in Caithness, although the pronunciation is closer to their reflex of MATE-HAME. In Shetland, *the* is regularly pronounced with initial /d/.

3.5 Adjectives

In general, our dialects realise adjectives in essentially the same way as Standard English. It should be noted, however, that while Standard English only uses the comparative suffix *-er* and the superlative suffix *-est* with adjectives of two syllables or less, many speakers of traditional Northern and Insular dialects use them with any adjective, no matter its number of syllables. Forms such as *beautifullest* are by no means uncommon. Double comparatives and superlatives, along the lines of *mair beautifuller*, are also not unknown. These features manifest themselves even in speech relatively close to the SSE end of the Scottish language continuum.

3.6 Verbs

3.6.1 Inflections

The ways in which Northern and Insular Scots express number and tense through verb inflections are not dissimilar to those found with other varieties of English. There is the same general drift from expressing past tense through vowel change (*strong verbs*) to the addition of a dental suffix (*weak verbs*) so that, for instance, Old English *he healp* is equivalent to Modern English *he helped*. There are, however, a number of occasions when our varieties (along with, often, other Scots varieties) differ from the Standard English inflectional pattern.

In the first place, a number of verbs which are 'irregular' in their past tense and past participle marking in Standard English have a regularised form in northern and insular dialects. Some 'strong' verbs in Standard English can be declined 'weak', so that the past tense of *give* (*gie* in Scots) is *gied* (sometimes *gaed* in the North East). The equivalent to *sold* is regularly *selt*, of *told*, *telt* (the change from /d/ to /t/ in these forms is discussed below; in Caithness, this change does not regularly take place).

Also observable are contexts where English does not mark the past at all but Scots does, so that the past tense and past participle of *hurt*, *hurt* in the standard, is *hurtit* to many Scots speakers.

A further distinction is where English uses the past tense of another verb, so that *go* has *went* as its past tense in the Standard, but traditional Scots varieties have *gaed* (regularly pronounced /gid/ in North East Scots and /gyd/ in Shetland).

The use of *went* as both past tense marker and past participle, common throughout the English-speaking world, is also regularly heard throughout our area, particularly in urban areas, but also by many younger speakers even in country districts. Similar observations can be made for the use of original past participles, such as *done* or *seen*, as past tense forms.

On occasion English has a 'reduced form' for a past tense (for instance, *heard*, /hɛrd/ in SSE), but traditional varieties will have a 'full form' (on this occasion, pronounced /hird/ or /herd/). A less obvious example of the same phenomenon is in the past tense and past participle of *say*, regularly pronounced /sed/, particularly in stressed contexts. Many speakers will use these forms even when consciously speaking 'English'.

On the other hand, there are a number of occasions where the most traditional speakers in our area will maintain distinctions in the marking of tense with verbs which have been 'regularised' in many other varieties. Thus, the past tense of *begin* may be *begood*, of *climb* (regularly pronounced /klɪm/), *clam*, of *drive*, *drave*. For the equivalent of *let – lat –* the past tense, at least in Shetland, can be *löt*, elsewhere, occasionally, *leet*; the past participle, quite commonly, *latten*. In the North-East, *begood*, while not exactly obsolete, is certainly not common and may be kept alive artificially by its use in songs and popular drama; the further north you travel, the more likely you are to hear this form used regularly in everyday speech, although it was not recognised by many Shetlanders in fieldwork carried out in 2005.

In Standard English, most verbs mark person (in the singular) and number distinctions in the present tense. Thus, the inflectional paradigm of *see* is:

Figure 3.1 The present-tense verb paradigm in Standard English

Person	Singular	Plural
First	I see	We see
Second	You see Archaic: thou seest	You see
Third	He/she/it sees	They see

In many non-standard varieties, these distinctions are not always fully represented. Thus, in non-standard Southern British English varieties, it is not unusual to hear someone say *you was* where the Standard would demand *you were*. In Northern England and Scotland, a different, but analogous, outcome is common: plural subjects can take what appear at surface level to be singular verbs.

There are some sub-rules to this *Northern Verb Concord Rule*. Plural personal pronouns generally only take verbs with plural forms; the use of 'singular' forms appears to be more common the more complex the subject is in terms of post-modification in particular: for instance, *The men we saw walkin doon the road is comin back*. All speakers, even when using the densest forms of traditional dialect, often shift unconsciously from 'standard' to 'non-standard' inflections throughout their speech. This apparent 'blurring' of the distinctions between singular and plural should be distinguished from (although it may sometimes unwittingly overlap) the use of *-s* with all numbers in what could be seen as a 'narrative' or 'past historic' tense, along the lines of 'So I walks into the pub and I says to the barman . . .', which is common in many varieties of English, including those under discussion here.

In the traditional dialects of the Northern Isles, where equivalents to (archaic) English *thou* are found, associated verbs take *-s* as the inflection, so that in Shetland, *du sees* would be equivalent to 'you [singular] see'.

In Standard English, the *-(e)d* ending marking past tense and past participles with the majority of verbs is generally pronounced [d], except when the ending follows a voiceless consonant, where devoicing occurs to [t], sometimes represented in the spelling (for instance, *leapt*), sometimes not (for instance, *reefed*). The distribution of /d/ and /t/ forms in our areas is similar, although more thorough-going. A further variant of *-ed* also occurs: /ɪt/.

Macafee (1992–) demonstrates that there is a threefold distribution based upon the context. /ɪt/ is most common 'after plosives and unstressed vowels', *A liftit me haan til'm*, 'I lifted my hand to him', i.e. 'I hit him'. /d/ is regular after vowels, as with *He gaed me sic a fricht*, 'he gave me such a fright', and is common in everyday speech after voiced fricatives: for instance, *The door wis closed*. In Caithness, forms with /t/ in other dialects are pronounced /d/, although a distinction is preserved between /d/ with no preceding vowel in the suffix and /ɪd/. Other varieties which border on the former Gaelic-speaking territory may also have either entirely voiceless or voiced consonants in all of these contexts.

3.6.2 Use of the progressive aspect

All varieties of Scots, as with English, overtly express the progressive aspect in present and past by a combination of the appropriate form of *be* and the present participle. Unlike Standard English, however, a number of stative verbs, which cannot be associated with overt progressive expression in that variety, have the possibility of progressive realisation in Scots. These include, in particular, *think, want* and *doubt. A wis thinkan that mebbe the morn wisna the best day fur deein it,* 'I don't think that tomorrow is the best day to do it'. This feature is used by speakers whether they are self-consciously using Scots or Standard English.

3.6.3 *Perfective aspect in Shetland*

In almost all of the varieties discussed in this book, *have* is used along with the past participle to express perfective aspect in expressions such as *he has finally arrived.* Perhaps the most striking structural feature of Shetlandic is the use of *be* as an auxiliary verb in active perfective constructions with all types of verbs.

Pavlenko (1997: 88) distinguishes three senses associated in standard English with *be* + past participle:

1. the function of the copula [a verb used to connect two phrases which are complementary to each other; the most common of these is *be*]: *He is changed* 'He is different';
2. the function of a perfective auxiliary (with intransitives [verbs which cannot take a direct object]): *He is changed* 'He has become different';
3. the function of a passive marker (with transitives [verbs which can take a direct object]): *He is changed* 'He has been made different [by an external force]'

Another sense is associated with Shetland dialect, Pavlenko notes:

4. the function of a perfective auxiliary both with intransitives and transitives: *He is changed* 'He has changed something or someone'

Examples of the construction are found (Robertson and Graham 1952: 11) in

Fifty voars I'm dell'd an set da tatties, 'I have sorted and planted the potatoes for fifty years [literally, fifty springs]'

or

When A'm feenished yun A'll be dön a göd day's wark, 'When I have finished that I will have done a good day's work'.

With this type of example it is very easy for non-Shetlanders to hear pro-gressive *A am döin,* for *A am dön,* or its equivalents. I was caught out by this on more than one occasion when carrying out fieldwork.

3.6.4 The infinitive

A relict feature in the speech of many inhabitants of northern Scotland and the Northern Isles is the use of *for to* (often *for tee/tae* or *for til*) as an infinitival form, generally distinguished semantically from the 'simple' *to* (*tee/tae, til*) by its greater overt expression of purpose. The Old Norse infinitival marker *at* is 'fossilised' in the form *adee* in the North-East (as in *Fit's adee wi ye?,* 'what's wrong with you?'). This is, of course, equivalent to Standard English *ado* (as in 'Much ado about nothing') but is much more of an active feature in local speech.

3.6.5 Verb negation

In English, the general trend over the last 600 years has been to use the *do*-periphrasis when a verb in simple present or past tense is found with a negator, rather than using a negative particle with the 'regular' form of the verb. Thus 'He laughed not' was replaced by 'He did not laugh'. Scots shares this development, using the *–na* suffix instead of SSE *'nt. He didna laach.*

The changeover from the earlier system to the present one is rela-tively recent in the most traditional dialects. On the east coast, the form for *do* in the present tense in these auxiliary contexts is often *div* /dɪv/.

The same switch from main verb use to *do*-periphrasis along with negation is to be found in questions. On this occasion, however, Macafee (1992–) reports that the old system is still functioning (or has only recently ceased to function) in Shetland dialect. In the other contempo-rary dialects, *-na* is combined regularly only with modal verbs (although this can be found in any negative context); in particular *can,* as with *Ye canna say that, min,* 'you can't say that, man', and *will,* as in *A winna dee't,* 'I won't do it'.

In a negative declarative sentence Standard English would normally associate the negator (particularly in contracted form) with the part of the verb which carries grammatical information, as with *I won't do it* (= I will not do it). This construction type is certainly possible in Scots (*A winna dee't*). More common, however, is the use of a free-standing negator following the part of the verb carrying grammatical informa-tion, as in *A'll nae dee't.* This feature is carried into Scottish English, with the substitution of *not* for the native isolated negator, thus making this an example of covert Scotticism. In North-East Scots, the negative particle is *nae* /ne/; in the rest of the North and in the Northern Isles, the equivalent, as with Central Scots, is *no* /no/.

As well as using a separable negative particle, all dialects of Scots employ an enclitic particle (a morpheme which is 'implanted' into the end of a word and cannot stand alone), *-na*, pronounced /nʌ/ or /nə/ in the areas under discussion. Historically, this could be added to any verb; remnants of this do persist in traditional dialects (*A daurna*, 'I don't dare to', seems particularly common in my experience), although this is often a cross-over from contemporary or, more often, historical literary usage.

In North-East Scots, expressions where the *do*-periphrasis appears to be deleted, along the lines of *You na ken aathin aboot me!*, 'you don't know everything about me' are common. Smith (2000) suggests reasons for this development.

In the same dialect, expressions such as *He's a gweed doctor, is he?*, using a positive tag question, do not necessarily request a genuine evaluation of the doctor's abilities as 'He's a good doctor, is he?' would in Standard English. Instead, the positive question tag expects a positive response equivalent to Standard English 'He's a good doctor, isn't he?' Very common even when locals are self-consciously speaking SSE, this usage often confuses incomers. Its distribution patterns are discussed by Amini (1998). The 'normal' *He's a gweed doctor, is he nae?* is regularly heard, however.

3.6.6 The modal verbs

Although all Scots varieties have the full set of English modal verbs, some are used in different semantic contexts from the usage of the Standard English of England and elsewhere.

Will (or its local variants) is used to express futurity with first person singular subjects. *Shall* is rarely used, except in careful speech when a particularly 'English' register is sought after in expressions such as 'They shall come tomorrow'. This construction appears to have its origin in school usage. The equivalent older Scots form *sal* is rarely heard now, although a contraction /z/ is current in literary North-East usage: *I'se see him the morn*.

As Miller (2003: 89–90) points out, *must* is only used to express conclusions (what linguists term *epistemic modality*), along the lines of *Ye must be back the morn if ye want tae see him*. Standard English (except in Scotland) can also use *must* to express obligation (*deontic* modality), so that 'You must be back tomorrow' would be interpreted as a requirement or order. Although there is some 'leakage' of this usage into Scottish speech, most speakers prefer *have to* or the more forceful *have got to* in these contexts: *Ye hiv tae be back the morn.* The Scots modal *maun* /mʌn/, often used in our area by older speakers, is generally also only used to express conclusions.

The 'double modal' construction, along the lines of *A'll can see him the morn*, common in Mid-Scots, is rarely if ever heard in Northern or Insular Scots.

3.7 Conclusion

What separates Northern and Insular Scots from Standard English in morphosyntactic terms is significantly less than is the case for either phonology or lexis. What divergence there is can be analysed in three ways. In the first place, as an area relatively distant from major population centres, associated until recently with traditional employment patterns, many grammatical features not shared with the Standard are relics of earlier usage. Moreover, there are occasions where Scots as a whole (as well as, on occasion, the northern dialects of English) employs a separate pattern to that found in southern dialects. Finally, there are those occasions where innovation appears to have been triggered in these areas, sometimes, it could be argued, because of substrate influences from languages previously spoken in the area. It might even be the case, as with the retention of a discrete second-person singular pronoun, or the lack of overt plural marking for *this* and *that*, that a combination of all these processes is present.

4 Lexis

4.1 Introduction

When I first moved to the North-East, I was struck by the 'richness' of the local dialect's vocabulary. Many words, such as *bide*, 'to reside', while known to me, were associated in my mind with the speech of my grandparents. I now heard them daily in the language of children and young adults. This is, in fact, a feature of all the Northern and Insular dialects: many of the words which make them distinctive were once common in other Scots dialects.

This does not mean, of course, that the various dialects do not have lexical features which make them distinctive in the eyes both of native speakers and outsiders. Indeed, there were – and are – certain words and phrases which act as shibboleths. *Peerie* (or *peedie*), 'small, little, young', is peculiarly a part of Insular and Caithness speech, although recognised by other northerners; *tyaave*, 'to struggle, exist, survive', is associated in particular with the North-East. Indeed, for the larger dialect areas, a veritable industry has come into being dedicated to the production of popular, or semi-scholarly, dictionaries and phrase books.

Nevertheless, our knowledge of the lexis actually used in particular places is often sketchy. This is especially the case with the less populous (and most threatened) dialects. What follows is therefore largely a work in progress and more anecdotal, personal and indicative than I would wish. I will nevertheless attempt to show how a close analysis of the evidence may lead us to a number of (tentative) conclusions about the particular semantic fields which are well-represented, along with explanations for the distinctiveness of local vocabulary.

4.2 Scholarly resources: national

The primary sources for the study of the recent and contemporary lexical patterns of Scots are the *Scottish National Dictionary* (*SND*) (Grant and Murison 1929–76) and the *Linguistic Atlas of Scotland* (Mather and Speitel 1975–85). Their discussion of lexical use across the country is scholarly and thorough. On the other hand, the surveys underlying the works (in particular the *Linguistic Atlas*) largely ignored urban areas, even though the ratio of urban to rural living is particularly weighted towards the former in Scotland. The means of reporting is heavily biased towards the most conservative forms of local speech; forms of speech which may not be representative of local language as a whole. In the case of the *SND* there is an inevitable concentration on contemporary and particularly historical literary use. Moreover, we are at the mercy of the skill of the collectors and the ability of informants. It is common for native speakers to know words which, according to these resources, would not be present in that area.

Nevertheless, when taken as a whole, the information provided both by the *Atlas* and the *Dictionary* can illustrate what we believe constitutes traditional Scots lexis in our areas.

Even a cursory consultation of the *Linguistic Atlas* suggests that patterns are discernible in the geographical distribution of particular words or meanings. There are occasions, such as for 'soap suds' (Mather and Speitel 1975–85: I, Map 14), where speakers in Orkney and Shetland use the same collocation ('[soapy] blots'), which is not shared by the Northern dialects. There are also occasions where speakers in the Northern Isles have the same – or similar – word or collocation as that found in northern Scotland, whether that be only part of the north, such as the North-East, for instance, in words concerned with 'down draught' (ibid.: I, Map 15), represented by *fla(w)n*) or as a whole. On other occasions, such as 'a stroke with the tawse [the leather strap used formerly in Scottish schools as a punishment]' (ibid.: I, Map 30), at least some of the Northern Isles share more in common with central Scots (often particularly Angus and Fife) in using *palmie* or *palm*, than they do with more northerly dialects, where *lick* or *skelp* are common. Occasionally, also, as with 'fowl dung' (ibid.: I, Map 68), the southern dialects of Shetland have more in common with Orkney (and often the Northern dialects), in using *dirt*, than they do with the more northern dialects of their own archipelago, where *scootings* or *scoot* is common. Sometimes, as with 'muck hoe' (ibid.: I, Map 41), Orkney, but not Shetland, is in line with northern Scotland in using (*byre*) *scra(p)per*. Sometimes each (or almost all) of the regions employs a different word or collocation for the same concept, as is the case, for instance, with 'ant' (ibid.: I, Map 76), with Shetland using *mooratoog*, Orkney *meeroo* and the North-East *eemert, emmet* or *emmerteen* (and its variants).

In the larger areas, such as the North-East, internal distinctions are present, as is the case with 'couch grass' (Mather and Speitel 1975–85: I,

Map 87): on this occasion between the north coast (along with the hinterland of the Deveron and Spey valleys), where *knot grass* is recorded, and the east coast, where *string grass* is cited. Very occasionally, as with 'hoar frost' (ibid.: II, Map 67), the area around the Beauly Firth is distinguished, in its use of *grey frost*, from all other Northern dialects. The most common pattern, however, is where a number of the Northern and Insular dialects share a distribution pattern which covers most of the Scots language area, whether patchily or generally, such as for 'three legged stool' (ibid.: I, Map 13), where *creepie* is the dominant form.

Similar patterns can be observed in the *SND* corpus, here cited in its readily accessible *Concise Scots Dictionary* form. There are some words or particular meanings found only in the Northern Isles and Northern Scotland, such as

> **forsta** *vt* understand *19-*, *Sh[etland] Ork[ney] Ab[er]d[eenshire]*.

Sometimes Caithness is singled out in relation to the Northern Isles, as with

> **peerie, peedie** *adj* small, little, tiny *la19-*, *now Sh[etland] Ork[ney] Cai[thness]*;

often, however, Shetland and Orkney stand alone, as with

> **pell**[1] *n, contemptuous* a dirty, worthless person, reprobate, tramp, *now Sh[etland] Ork[ney]*,

or even one archipelago has unique usage, as with

> **hank**[2] *chf in pl or* **fore** or **aft** ~(s) the places on each side of a boat where the sideboards come together at stem or stern, the quarters *la16-*, *now Sh[etland]*.

There are also a wide range of vocabulary items, such as

> **stathel** *n* 2. the main part of a cornstack; a stack in the process of building or dismantling *17-*, *now local N[orthern Scotland]*,

which are (fairly) general to the northern counties. The North-East has many usages peculiar to itself, however, as with

> **lewder** *n* 1. a wooden lever, *esp* one for lifting millstones *la16-*, *now N[orth]E[ast]*,

as does Caithness, for instance

> **ranter** *vt* sew together, darn, mend *17-, now Cai[thness]*,

and the area around the Beauly Firth, as with

> **potch potch** *interj., also* ~**ie** ~**ie** a call to a pig *la20-, Ross Inv[ernessshire] Nai[rnshire]*.

There are also occasions where areas within the North-East diverge from each other, as in

> **doublet** *n* 2. *in pl* clothes, garments *19-, now B[a]nf[fshire]*.

More common, however, is a pattern where some Northern and Insular dialects have similar usage to the Southern and Central dialects, as with

> **lift**[2] *vt* 4.(1) (b) *specif of a sheep-dog* round up (sheep) and move them forward *20- now Ork[ney] Fif[e] K[irk]c[ud]b[right]*

or

> **first** ~ **fit** n 1. the first person (or animal) met on a journey, *esp* by a wedding or a christening party on the way to church *18-, now Cai[thness] Ab[er]d[een-shire] St[ir]l[in]g.*

Often the description of use is general for almost all of Scotland; nevertheless, there are a significant number of occasions (as with the above) where only parts of the more southern areas are mentioned. As I showed in Millar (1999), it is not unusual to find lexical items still in contemporary or recent use in both the north and south of Scotland, with only historical usage, if that, reported for the centre. Thus, for instance, according to the *SND* (s.v. *cleek*), the term *cleek anchor* for a small anchor is confined nowadays to Caithness and Kirkcudbright; one of the meanings of *mell*, 'to concern or busy oneself improperly or intrusively [*chf* **with** an affair, action; goods, property; a person]' is presently confined to Shetland, Kirkcudbright and Selkirk. Indeed, this view is supported by the regular use of *now* in many *Concise Scots Dictionary* entries, suggesting a previously wider usage pattern.

Details of this kind are difficult to follow. Regularising a little, the following patterns, sometimes overlapping, can be suggested:

1. The Northern Isles dialects have a common usage not employed by speakers of the mainland Northern dialects.
2. Northern and Insular dialects act as a bloc in distinction to other dialects.
3. Caithness dialect is part of a bloc with the Northern Isles dialects, but is separate from the other mainland Northern dialects.
4. Northern Isles dialects and some Northern dialects have lexical features in common which they do not share with other Northern dialects.
5. A Northern feature is found with some Insular dialects, but not others.
6. The dialects of the Northern Isles and the east-central counties of Scotland (Angus, Fife and the Lothians) share usage. This usage is not found in the mainland Northern dialects.
7. All Scots dialects share lexical features; the words and phrases involved are more common in the Northern Isles and northern Scotland, however.

Which patterns are dominant is, as yet, impossible to say. These trends will be discussed further into this chapter, as well as in Chapter 5.

4.3 Locally focused resources

These national resources, no matter their scholarly quality, cannot, nor were intended to, present a full picture of local usage. Nor can they tell us what semantic fields are best represented in what areas or what local people consider important and distinctive about their dialect. We must turn, therefore, to more localised dictionaries, glossaries and wordlists which have been produced for various dialects within our region. It should be noted, however, that the quality of these works (not necessarily in scholarly terms) is highly variable.

Shetland, for instance, is particularly well-represented, since the vocabulary of its dialect has been discussed in a scholarly manner on two occasions with a considerable time-gap between them: Jakobsen (1932; research carried out in the 1890s) and Graham (1993). Changes in Shetland lexis, as recognised by these dictionaries, will be discussed in Chapter 5.

When we compare the material in Graham (1993) and that found in the *SND* corpus, it is apparent that the vocabulary items he reports can be separated into three groupings. First, a large part of the vocabulary is common to many (if not all) dialects of Scots, or was until relatively recently, although naturally reported in a Shetland form. Thus *blöd-freends*, 'close friends, relatives', can be related to *bluid-friends*, as reported in the *SND*. On occasion, semantic extension has taken place. For instance, *draig*, defined by Graham as 'a dredge, especially used by fishermen for collecting **yoags** (large mussels)', appears to be an extension in meaning of *drag*, the second meaning for which in the *SND* is 'a large heavy harrow', reported since the late nineteenth century (the maritime connection is also made in the third *SND* meaning, which refers to 'the motion of the tide'). Another example of this may be *frush*, defined by Graham as 'to splutter or spit, as an angry cat; to spurt'. In the *SND* this particular meaning does not exist for this word; on the other hand, there are a number of meanings, associated only with adjectival function, which appear to be related to it:

> 1 *of pastry etc* crisp, short, crumbly *18-*, *now Ork[ney] S[outh]W[est]*. 2 *of soil* crumbly, loose *19-*, *now local Ork[ney]-D[u]mf[iesshire]*. 3 *of wood, vegetable fibre, cloth etc* brittle, apt to disintegrate, decayed, rotten *la18-*, *local Ork[ney]-D[u]mf[iesshire]*. 4 frank, bold rash *la18-e20* 5 tender, easily hurt or destroyed *19-e20*

Thus Shetland lexis can be analysed as an integral part of the Scots lexical continuum. Developments – both in meaning and form – peculiar to Shetland are also common, however, establishing the local dialect's distinctiveness.

Graham also reports the use of words which the *SND* does not associate with Shetland. A good example of this is *dungeon*, defined by Graham as 'applied to someone who has great knowledge. *He wis jöst a dungeon o lear*', literally, 'he was just a dungeon of learning'. The *SND* states that this particular meaning is '*local B[a]nf[fshire]-K[irk]c[ud]b[right]*'. This illustrates a problem which even the most dedicated lexicographer has: you are only as good as your sources. Sometimes a word is well-known in a particular place, but has never been recorded.

There are, however, a considerable number of items – probably more than half of the total collection – which are recorded in Graham, but not in the *SND*. Many of these refer to local flora or fauna, such as

> **banks-flooer** (n) sea-pink (*Armeria maritima*)

or the traditional ways of life of the archipelago, as, for instance,

> **fastibaand** (n) a cross-beam running under the thwarts of a boat to secure the frames.

Other overlooked items deal with the everyday perception of life, such as

ormal (n) a particle, a scrap. Usually in plural form, meaning remainder. *Dey wir naethin left ida biscuit tin but da ormals o a Digestive.* ['There was nothing left in the biscuit tin but the crumbs of a digestive']

or

blinnda (n) a mixture of grains of poor quality,

as well as words expressing everyday activities, such as

yarg (v) to complain incessantly; to carp *I wis hid anyoch o his yargin at never aesed* ['I had had enough of his constant complaining which never eased off']. (n) incessant complaining and criticising.

As will be discussed in Chapter 5, the fact that these words and meanings refer to the everyday lives and occupations of most residents of Shetland is significant. When the perception of this life and work is local – a viewpoint encouraged by island life – the local language variety will bear evidence of such a concentration.

Although, probably unfairly, Marwick's *Orkney Norn* (1929) is sometimes considered a poor companion to Jakobsen's equivalent survey of Shetland vocabulary, Orkney is nonetheless blessed in having a particularly impressive dictionary of the modern dialect by Lamb (1988). Lamb's work is especially helpful because it gives etymologies of most words as well as using symbols for moribund usages and for the most commonly used words. Using this information along with material from the *SND* corpus, I will present a brief discussion of some of the semantic fields to which specifically Orcadian words, defined by Lamb as being frequently used, belong.

Household words such as *baak*

baak, bauk 1. a rafter, usually COUPLE BAAKS or TWART-BAAKS 2. a hen's roost [also Sh(etland)] 3. a rope from which nets are hung 4. the line from which hooks are suspended 5. a seat in a boat 6. a ridge in ploughing 7. a division between lands 8. a low partition wall in Orkney houses baakhuins, baakheuns, to be *in the baak heuns* means to be out of sorts or offended [the essential meaning is to stay on the perch like a sick hen] [ON *bjálki* a beam or *bálkr* a partition]

are certainly found in the *Wordbook*, and a number of agricultural words, such as

netting wire wire netting [an example of many inverted phrases in Orkney dial(ect) . . .],

are cited. It is nevertheless striking that there are fewer common Orkney-specific terms referring to the farming life and its experience than is the case for Shetland. This may be due to chance; certainly the present evidence does not allow for any true conclusion. Nevertheless, this discrepancy might indicate that the proximity of Orkney to the Scottish mainland, along with its similar environment, could produce a similarity in farming practice over an extended period, along with terminological homogenisation for these practices. Indeed, *baak*, along with its agricultural associations, has a number of meanings connected to fishing. This semantic extension may explain why the word has been maintained. The original domestic meaning might have been retained because of the extension's connection with a distinctive part of Orcadian life.

This view is supported by the fact that the semantic fields of fishing and its related experiences possess a number of words which are not found in northern Scotland, such as

andoo 1. to row a boat against wind or tide so that it keeps in position for fishing etc. 2. to stroll [ON *andoefa* to keep a boat in position by rowing; also Sh(etland)]

An extension of meaning is present not, as we might normally expect, from land-based experience to sea-based, but rather vice versa.

There are also a considerable number of words concerned with marine fauna, many of which are derived from Norn and, like the previous example, are shared with Shetland, such as

bonxie the great skua [also Sh(etland); ON *bunki* a heap; the reference being to its size]

or

piltick a second year coalfish [also Sh(etland); ON *piltr* boy]

Beyond this, a number of common action verbs, such as

drock *a drock o swaet* saturated in perspiration. *drockin* a drenching. *drockit, drockéd, drockled, draigelt. like a drockled rat* very wet, drenched [related to ON *drukna* to be drowned] or

> **moor** 1. of snow, to drift 2. a thick blinding snowstorm: *moored wi the cowld* having difficulty in breathing because of a heavy cold [Icel(andic) *mor* dust; Norw(egian) *mure* coal refuse . . .]

are considered frequent. Both words represent a cross-over point between Norn and Scots. With *drock*, the past participle form *draigelt* is a common Scots word (and related to English *bedraggled*); *drockled* could be seen as a half-way house between the Norn and Scots forms. With *moor*, some of the meanings associated with it – particularly those to do with stifling or suffocation – appear to be partial transfers from the similar Scots verbs *smoor* and *smore*. A closer long-term relationship between the two languages than was the case elsewhere can be postulated. This point will be returned to in Chapter 5.

As with Shetland, it appears that words and phrases associated with what was until recently the local way of life are most likely to be distinctive to the area and to have survived best.

The North-East is not as well-served by scholarly or popular discussion of local lexis. Indeed, the only true dictionary is Kynoch (2004), which is both an historical dictionary (giving definitions for words and phrases employed by writers from the North-East in the nineteenth and early twentieth centuries) and an attempt to record contemporary usage. Unlike Lamb, no information on regularity of usage is given; unlike the Shetland evidence discussed above, most of the words and phrases found in Kynoch are also found in the *SND*. It does act as a short-cut, however, demonstrating what a perceptive native considers specifically local usage. It is impressive that a large part of his material is representative of a peculiarly Northern vocabulary, therefore.

A number of these items refer to the life of the land; in particular farming. One of these is *hummel-doddie*, used to refer to hornless cattle in traditional dialects from Caithness to Angus. Interestingly, Kynoch demonstrates that an extension of meaning not specifically referred to in the *SND* is present: *hummel-doddies* can refer to woollen mittens without fingers. I have heard this used by speakers who had no connection to farming and no idea that it was employed originally with reference to cattle.

A collocation not found in the *SND* is *lowsin-shooer*, a 'heavy shower of rain putting a stop to outdoor work on farm' (although the word *lowse*, referring to the cessation of work, is a common Scots word). As with many of Kynoch's more evocative words and phrases, this phrase is derived from Buchan and Toulmin (1989), an excellent wordlist collated by two local writers immediately connected throughout their working lives to the region's traditional occupations.

Also connected to the country life are the many local words for flora and fauna. One example of this is *teuchat*, 'lapwing'. The phrase *teuchat's storm*, referring to 'the wintry weather in March, when the lapwings arrive', is, according to the *SND*, confined to the North-East and the counties of Angus and Perthshire.

Kynoch also includes a number of local words and phrases referring to the fishing industry, many of which were peculiar to particular ports or stretches of coastline, and will be discussed in section 4.4 and Chapter 5. One of the most evocative is also derived from Buchan and Toulmin's collection: *black-yarn*, referring to empty herring nets. Again, the traditional way of life of the region is well represented in its distinctive vocabulary.

As with most non-standard varieties of English, many of the words which survive best in the North-East refer to personality traits (often faults), as can be seen with *aetmeat*, defined by Kynoch (2004) as 'one who eats without working', and by the *SND* as a 'parasite'. Its use is confined to Banffshire and Aberdeenshire. Other words, such as *news*, a noun and verb for to chat or gossip, largely confined to Shetland and the northern dialects, or *yokie*, 'itchy' or 'scratchy', found in most northern dialects, are still used and understood in the area.

A feature which marks off North-East Scots from other mainland varieties is its divergent phonology. This means that many of the words and phrases in Kynoch (2004) are to be found in other parts of Scotland, such as *wyve* 'weave'; their relationship to the forms found in other dialects is not always transparent, however. On occasions, in fact, the SSE and local pronunciations of a word both exist, with a distinction in meaning developed between the alternative pronunciations. A resident of Lossiemouth informed me that, in her Moray dialect, the word *weaken* had its Standard sense of loss of strength when pronounced with /i/, but could mean 'not quite right', perhaps implying a lessening in moral behaviour, when the local /e/ pronunciation was employed.

The lexical items Kynoch cites very often refer to a passing way of life, however, as with *bar-fit broth*, 'soup made without meat'. In his work, as well as in the *SND*, the level of lexis which survived in the North-East at least into living memory referring to older cultural traditions is impressive. This can be seen in reference to *Auld Eel*, 'Old Yule', the celebration of Christmas according to the Julian calendar, *Fastern's Een*, 'Shrove Tuesday', and *Pace*, 'Easter', particularly in the combination *Pace eggs*. This retention can also be found in the occasional use of *Feersday* for Thursday and the use of *half* in time phrases such as *half five* to refer to the preceding rather than coming hour (so that this particular example would represent the same time as *half past four* in Standard British English). This form of time-marking is the norm for all other Germanic languages. Impressive though this retention may be, it stills leaves large parts of the vocabulary open to being perceived as old-fashioned.

Beyond these resources, a number of scholars have also discussed the lexis of this region. McClure (1987: 313), for instance, points out that:

> The copious and fascinating literature of the North-east ... attests to the remarkable richness and distinctiveness of the local dialect vocabulary. Not only in the works of William Alexander, Charles Murray and their successors, but in the speech of rural and coastal Aberdeenshire until well within living memory, local words could be heard in abundance: a couple of dozen selected almost at random are *baillie* (cattleman), *boodie* (goblin, or scarecrow), *brodmill* (brood of chickens), *clossach* (hoard of money), *clyack-sheaf* (last sheaf cut at harvest), *dundeerie* or *dinnideer* (uproar), *feer* (plough the first guiding furrow), *galshach* (a delicacy), *gansey* or *maasey* (a thick woollen jersey), *gudge* (short thick-set person), *habber* (stutter), *hallach* (scatterbrained), *keb* (sheep tick), *kink-hoast* (whooping cough), *raeverie* (rumour), *squallach* (scream), *stamagaster* (unpleasant surprise), *thraaheuk* (instrument for twisting straw ropes), *yaavins* (bristles of barley), *yowies* (fir cones). Undoubtedly there are many people still alive in Aberdeenshire who have some or all of these words in their active vocabulary, and many more for whom they are at least a living memory.

It is striking that large elements of this highly distinctive vocabulary is associated with occupations which were formerly dominant in the region – fishing and farming – but which are now much sidelined (in the case of farming) or practically moribund (in the case of fishing).

McClure recognises that many of these words would now be unknown to younger, particularly urban, North-Easterners. Indeed, he laments the passing of the 'pristine rural and coastal dialects of Aberdeenshire' (McClure 1987: 314). He does, however, note (ibid.: 314) that Aberdeen City has its own distinctive vocabulary:

> Schoolboys play marbles with such diverse varieties as *dazzies, peezies, peebles* and *tattie-smashers*, using as targets *kypies* (depressions in the ground) or *fennies* (the action of standing with heels together and toes apart). A ride on some-body's back is a *coalie-bag* – a term which, without the diminutive, even finds its way into school sports-day programmes – and a ride on the shoulders is a *coxie-cusie* or *cockerty-hooie*. An ice-cream cone is a *cappie* – a peculiar local development of the general Scots word *cap* or *caup* meaning a wooden dish. Rubber-soled training shoes are *jimmies*, presumably from *gym-shoes*: if an

Edinburgher in Aberdeen asked for them by his local word *gutties* he would be given golf-balls. Boot polish is *blaik* and laces are *pynts*.

Aberdeen bakers deal in *rowies* (crisp flaky rolls: the word, of course, is the Scots cognate of *roll* with the usal diminutive suffix but its use is specifically restricted to this particular type of roll), *safties* (*softies* to the more genteel – soft rolls) and *stewie-baps* (floured rolls – hence the taunt 'Ye couldna knock the stew aff a bap!' *Stew* is not generally used of flour except in this context: its usual meaning is dust). The amateur gardeners whose efforts are such an asset to Aberdeen fertilise their plots with *sharn* (manure) and water them from *roozers* (watering cans). Fractious children *wheenge* and *peenge*. To trip over your own feet is to *hyter*, to play aimlessly with something is to *ficher*, to work in an ineffectual, disorganised fashion is to *scutter*. *Bam, bampot* and *bam-stick* are common insult terms denoting lack of intelligence.

Although some of these terms, such as *bampot*, are common to many Scots dialects, many of these examples are peculiarly North-Eastern. The sense of a vibrant dialect-speaking community is very evident. The same is true for glossaries and discussions compiled by and for local people, such as the excellent *Lossie Glossie* of Lossiemouth, where a tang of the seaborne life is present. As Chapter 5 will show, however, recent changes to the economic and cultural basis of the region have seriously undermined this survival, placing dialect vocabulary of this type in a potentially perilous heritage niche.

Caithness is even less well-served, the only work aiming to be more than a word list being Sutherland (1992), compiled by a local historian and author. Unfortunately, this brief work contains little or no information on usage and provenance of the words defined, the compiler (ibid.: 7) merely stating in his introduction that:

> No one person would naturally have a vocabulary as wide as that to be found in this book, as townspeople would not be familiar with the wild flowers or wild-life. Similarly country dwellers would have no need for words used connected with the fishing industry.
>
> However all the words were spoken at one time or another, and I have heard nearly all of them over the last 20 years, used by the 70 or so people with whom I made tape recordings when I was preserving the different accents of Caithness.

The actual definitions of the words are also brief. Nevertheless, the book remains a useful source of both local lexis and pronunciations.

Inevitably, there are a considerable number of words for local flora and fauna, some of which, such as *doo-docken*, 'coltsfoot', are reinforced as being specific to Caithness by the *SND*. *Crottie*, defined by Sutherland as 'red lichen', appears to be a diminutive of *crottle*, 'dye-producing lichen', a word found throughout Scotland and derived from Gaelic *crotal*. These patterns are found throughout the book.

Words related to farming include *nask*, 'chain, usually in a byre', a word which is not present in the *SND*, and *meels*, 'crumbled earth, peat', representing a local pronunciation of the common Scots *muild*.

At least in this dictionary, these farming words seem in the minority in comparison to words associated with the fishing trade. The latter include *farlan*, defined by Sutherland as 'trough for ungutted herring'. The *SND* informs us that the word is found in this meaning in Shetland, Northern Scots, Fife and Berwickshire. It originates in Shetland, where the *foreland* was where fish-curing took place. Again we have witness of the close connections engendered by the herring fishery in particular. *Graith*, defined by Sutherland as 'foam on sea, soap suds', appears to be an example of a semantic transference not completely recognised by the *SND*. The primary meaning of this word is 'liquor, medicine'; subsidiary meanings include 'soapy lather' and 'stale urine', both of which contain the sense of foam. A taste of the seaborne life of the past can be found in *Mither o' the waters*, 'permanent on-shore swell off the east coast'.

Sutherland defines *could iron* as 'salmon'. The *SND* informs us that this phrase is part of the *tabu* language of fishermen (which will be discussed in 4.4), used 'when one of the prohibited terms has been uttered'. It may be that, as regularly happens with euphemisms, the original avoidance word has been transferred to the concept intended for avoidance. Another example associated with local folklore and tradition is *foregang*, 'apparition', which the *SND* informs us is associated with a premonition of death or other misfortune and found in Shetland, Caithness and Banffshire.

There are a number of words, such as *knappel*, 'youth', and *maggoty*, 'full of whims; unpredictable', which are not cited for Caithness in the *SND*, although they are found in more southerly dialects of Scots. Whether this represents an oversight on the part of the national project or an importation from literary usage on the part of Sutherland is impossible to tell.

The only wordlist I have been able to find for North Northern A is King Sutherland (no date), a private publication largely concerned with local folklore. A number of the words included there, such as *mugalees*, 'to destroy, make a mess of', do not appear to have been recorded by SND. The few words treated, along with the highly divergent pronunciations suggested by its orthography, makes it particularly sad that a more scholarly investigation into the Black Isle dialects was not undertaken when there were still considerable numbers of speakers.

While the material presently to hand cannot hope to produce robust usage patterns, the extent to which distinctive local words refer to the local traditional way of life is indicative. Given the ecologies of the areas involved, it is not surprising that many of the local words refer to farming or fishing. A possible distinction in pattern might be made, however, between the distribution of farming words and those associated with fishing. The latter, at least on occasion, appear to be found in a wide range of coastal regions both within our area and elsewhere. The peripatetic nature of the herring fishery is a possible source for this distribution.

4.4 Dialect vocabulary and heritage

As has been noted in the above, one of the striking features of all these dialects is the extent to which some of their most distinctive lexical items are associated with the former primary occupations of the region.

Thus, in the North-East of Scotland, we find many words associated with former agricultural methods, as discussed and analysed by Fenton (1987); indeed, Fenton's study demonstrates the level to which day-to-day life in traditional farming communities was described, in fact experienced, almost exclusively using local words. The same can be said to be true for the fishing trade. Downie (1983), in her discussion of the dialects of the Moray Firth fishing communities, demonstrates that, while much specialist vocabulary was common along these coasts, often each village would have local shibboleth forms to express identity:

> In the Moray area the word used [for 'seagull'] is *gow* or *seagow*, which are words most commonly used throughout the North East. Hopeman also added the name *gru willie* for 'a young gull'. Moving eastwards along the coast we meet a variety of words. A Fraserburgh word is *myave* given by one informant, while a different person also from Fraserburgh cited *scurrie*. *Scurrie* is also said in Peterhead. One informant gave me the word *pewlie* stating that it belonged to quite a precise area – Pennan, west of Fraserburgh. The Linguistic Atlas of Scotland shows an Aberdeen distribution for this word while the S[cottish] N[ational] D[ictionary] gives quotations from Banff. But in support of the response I was given the SND also states that the name *pewlie* is 'sometimes applied as a nickname to inhabitants of some of the remote Buchan fishing villages perched on or overhung by cliffs, e.g. Pennan'.

While some of this vocabulary has survived well, as I found when conducting fieldwork in Moray, an informant in Unst in Shetland suggested that younger people in his community no longer had the range of words formerly used to refer to different stages in animals' life cycles. When the way of life associated with the exploitation of these resources begins to fade, this complexity is no longer necessary.

Beyond this, a particularly interesting feature of many of our dialects is the use, at least until recently, by fishermen when on board their vessels of nicknames or pseudonyms to 'disguise' everyday persons, items and topics. This habit is not, of course, confined to fisher folk in northern Scotland and the Northern Isles. Even with the benefits of modern technology, there is always the threat of disaster and death. In the past, this was even more the case. It is not surprising that those involved in such a dangerous but vital occupation should develop a means of avoiding mentioning beings, objects or concepts considered unlucky. It is striking, in fact, that so many of these *tabus* are related to matters which would cause worry on the part of the fisher folk that they would either 'call up' the phenomenon in question (such as bad weather) or stop it from happening (as with good weather), or are related too closely with life on the land (for instance, domestic animals).

Other features might have encouraged the retention of this tradition. Fisher folk have traditionally been somewhat separate from their land-based neighbours, often marrying only within the fishing trade (although not necessarily from their own port) and conversing almost exclusively with people from your own background. As Dorian (1981), in her exploration of the death of Gaelic in East Sutherland, points out, the linguistic peculiarities of the fisher population were in part caused by prejudice felt against them but also through their own wish to maintain their group identity. The need to mark distinctiveness in what was often a rather adversarial world and (perhaps) to make discussion of certain topics difficult for outsiders to follow, probably encouraged the development of this special vocabulary. A particularly impressive development of this type was developed in Hopeman on the Moray coast, where *Hopeman Gaelic*, a form of back slang, was used between fishermen.

The phenomenon of *tabu* language is best covered for Orkney and Shetland. Fenton (1968–9; 1978) provides an extensive list of the semantic fields most closely associated with this special register. Significantly, many of these 'alternative' words and phrases are derived from the Scandinavian dialects previously spoken in the islands. One term for 'religious minister' is particularly interesting, since it was recorded in two forms, one Norse (*upstaar*), the other the Scots equivalent (*upstander*), apparently the more recent form. This suggests that some of the Norse items were becoming opaque for modern speakers of the dialect. The use of so many Norn words, only found in these contexts, will be returned to in Chapter 5.

A further example of the use of special terms in the fishing industry, on this occasion in the North-East, can be found in the tradition of *tee-names*, descriptive nicknames given to members of the community because of potential confusion between different people with the same name, a very common problem in tight-knit communities. A contributor to the entry for Rathen in Aberdeenshire in the third *Statistical Account of Scotland* (written in the 1950s), states that:

> In the following villages there is a great predominance of one or two surnames, namely Buchan, Duthie, Stephen: to overcome the difficulty of identification, each person has a 'tee-name' by which to be known. As an example of how the 'tee-names' are handed down – an old man, George, is known as 'Dancer's Dodie'; his son, Andrew, is 'Dancer's Dodie's Andreuchie' and then the grandson is 'Dancer's Dodie's Andreuchie's boy'. A man's 'tee-name' may even derive from his mother-in-law, as in the case of 'Beldie's Willie'. (Hamilton 1960: 323)

Although memories of this tradition remain, the post-war diversification in experience and naming tradition has rendered its purpose redundant. Similar naming practices were also prevalent on the Black Isle (King Sutherland, no date).

Again changes in work patterns and greater mobility are particularly dangerous to local usages of this type.

4.5 Discussion

What information can these national and local surveys give us on regional lexical choice? In the first place, much of the vocabulary of the Northern and Insular dialects is probably common to the more traditional dialects of the rest of Scotland. There are, however, occasions when specific words or collocations are confined to our area. It would be impossible to estimate the extent to which this pattern has been caused by the 'retreat' of an originally more widespread usage into the most traditional speech communities or whether they have always been confined to the North: both processes have probably been brought to bear on different usages.

Within our area, some lexical items or meanings are confined to one region, whether this be the North East, Caithness, the Northern Isles or parts thereof. There are only a few occasions where the Black Isle and its environs use lexical items which are entirely distinct from the more widespread dialects of the north. The same probable forces of change are to be found with these sub-areas as with the area as a whole. Although not fully quantifiable, it does seem that the Northern Isles are often distinctive in relation to the rest of the area; this distinctiveness is, on occasion, matched by correspondences *not* with the dialects of northern Scotland, but rather with the dialects of the eastern parts of the Central Belt.

It is striking that many of the most distinctive words and phrases are associated with traditional ways of life. As we will see in Chapter 5, changes in the structure of society and the employment opportunities now present may not augur well for the future survival of this distinctiveness. There is a particular danger of *heritigisation*, the survival of a limited number of vocabulary items in an essentially artificial cultural niche which may not be closely connected to the present everyday experience of locals.

This 'retreat' is not the whole story, however. Other factors must have collaborated in making these dialects so lexically distinctive. One possible explanation is that they have been influenced by other languages; it is to the idea of lexical borrowing that we will now turn.

4.6 Lexical borrowing

Although contemporary Scots dialects exhibit lexis borrowed from other languages independently from Standard English, from French (for instance *ashett*, 'large plate'), Low German or Dutch (such as *loon*, 'lad, boy') and Latin (whether legal terms, such as *propone*, 'propose', or everyday usages such as *stravaig*, 'walk'), and other languages, the primary external influences on the dialects of northern Scotland and the Northern Isles are Gaelic and Norse. Anticipating the discussion in Chapter 5, the following section will discuss these influences on dialect lexis.

4.6.1 Gaelic influence

Since Gaelic is so associated with Scottish cultural identity, with many ancient settlements bearing Gaelic names, it would be reasonable to expect that Scots would come under considerable influence from this language as speakers moved from one to the other, in ways not dissimilar to those suggested for many varieties of the English of Ireland (as discussed, for instance in Filippula 1999). Yet this did not happen, as Macafee and Ó Baoill (1997) have pointed out. There are a number of Gaelic words found in Scots but not English (or attested first in Scots, only to be borrowed into English later); the overwhelming majority of these – *glen* and *strath* for different kinds of valleys, *clabbydoo* for a particular type of mussel, *clachan* for a (small) village, being particularly common and striking examples – refer to topographical features or flora and fauna. This set is analogous to the few borrowings from British (the ancestor of modern Welsh, Cornish and Breton) the Anglo-Saxons adopted in their conquest of south-eastern Britain, as well as to the Native American words which English and French speakers assimilated in North America.

This type of influence is associated with typical forms of colonial settlement, where new animals and plants, as well as topographical features (including the names of places and rivers) are all that is needed by settlers before they dispossess the previous settlers. It does not presume lengthy or intimate contact. But since it is likely that, in the case of Scotland, most of the speakers of the local language remained as a peasantry in a new social situation, we can also glean information on the sociolinguistic relationship between the two languages during the transfer period. Outside what remained of the *Gaidhealtachd*, the Gaelic-speaking area, in the eighteenth century, the language had little or no prestige. This subsidiary status is reinforced by the prevalence of borrowings (such as *tocher*, 'bride-price') which refer to Gaelic cultural traditions and artefacts which are either foreign (and therefore exotic) to the majority of Lowland Scots speakers or which have been adopted as symbolic of a broader Scottish cultural distinctiveness.

Using the materials available from the *SND* corpus, it soon becomes apparent that there are, however, a number of regions of Scotland where Gaelic words have been borrowed rather more regularly, and without evidence in other dialects. The patterns involved are expressed in the following figure; the thicker the line, the greater the intensity of influence (see figure 4.1).

Those areas where lexical transfer is common must represent places where longer and more intimate language contact situations were present in the past. This might be due to the area in question being on the edge of a previously Gaelic-speaking area (such as Perthshire), for instance, *sownack*, 'bonfire; a heavy bog-fir torch used in Halloween fires', from Gaelic *samhnag*, 'Halloween bonfire', being where many Gaelic-speakers have migrated (such as Glasgow), as with *geenyoch*, 'ravenous, voracious, greedy', from Gaelic *gionach*, or being where Gaelic was spoken until relatively recently (such as south-western Scotland), with words like *gourlins*, 'the edible roots or tubers of the earth-nut', from Gaelic *cuthurlan* 'earth nut', or continues to be spoken in pockets (such as Argyll), for instance, *goich*, 'a haughty carriage of the head', from Gaelic *goic*, 'a tossing of the head'.

Figure 4.1 Levels of Gaelic lexical influence upon the dialects of Scots. Full lines imply primary contact; broken lines imply secondary contact. The thicker the line, the more intense the contact was.

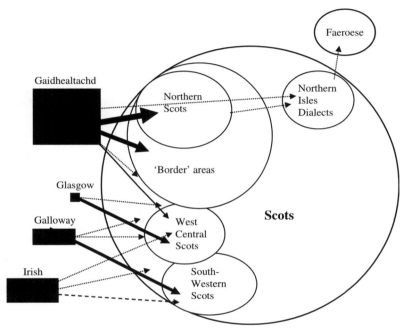

On occasion, a word can be found in a variety of places on this 'border', as with *doorie* 'a pig; the smallest pig of a litter', derived from Gaelic *durradh*, 'a pig, sow', possibly via *durrag*, 'a little pig'. distributed, at least until recently, across Argyll, South-Western Scotland and Ulster, often including areas concentrated upon in this book, for example *trooshlach*, 'trash, worthless things or people', found in Aberdeenshire, Angus and Wigtownshire, from Gaelic *trusdaireachd*, 'trash, dirt'. It should be noted that the word, when used as an adjective, meaning 'dirty, slovenly', is used only in the North-East. On these occasions this distribution may be due to 'retreat' into more traditional dialect areas (as discussed above), to mutual influence (perhaps due to the fishery) or to independent borrowing.

As will be shown in greater detail in Chapter 5, a large part of this 'border' area is to be found in the northern mainland of Scotland. It is unsurprising, therefore, that many Gaelic borrowings are peculiar to these areas. Looking at the North-East in the first place, we find words which refer to flora and fauna, such as *dirken*, 'fir-cone (used in smoking fish)', from Gaelic *duircean*; topographical terms, such as *ess*, 'waterfall', from Gaelic *eas*; terms referring to the outdoor, particularly agricultural, life, for instance, *skathie*, 'a rough shelter, especially a fence or wall used as a windbreak in front of a door', a diminutive form from Gaelic *sgàth*, 'a wattle fence or door; a shelter'; words referring to traditions, such as *clyack*, 'the last sheaf of corn of the harvest, dressed as a girl or decorated with ribbons' (from Gaelic *caileag*, 'girl'), which, by extension, came to mean the harvest-home supper for which the corn-dolly was prepared; also, terms of abuse, such as *wisgan*, 'a stunted, useless, feckless person or creature', probably from Gaelic *ùruisgean*, the diminutive form of *uruisg*, 'brownie, hobgoblin'.

A sub-class of these are words referring to aspects of the fishery, including *melg*, 'the milt of a male fish', derived from Gaelic *mealg*. Within the North-East, words from these and related semantic fields are found in more restricted areas (at least in recent times), including *boodie*, 'a ghost, hobgoblin', probably derived from Gaelic *bodach*, meaning the same thing, or *fuilteach*, 'the weather occurring in a period at least partly in February, of varying date and duration', recorded in Aberdeenshire and Banffshire, from Gaelic *faoilteach*, 'the last fortnight of winter and the first of summer, usually a period of stormy weather', *gnashick*, 'the red bearberry', from Gaelic *cnàimhseag*, found in Morayshire and Banffshire, and *drone* (< Gaelic *dronn*), 'the buttocks', found in Angus. Interestingly there is at least one example of Gaelic borrowing or influence where the word in question, *cameral*, 'a haddock after spawning', seems to be derived from an Irish, rather than Scottish, source, *camramhail*, 'dirty'.

A rather greater number of Gaelic borrowings are to be found for Caithness, including *boch*, 'a child's toy, a knick-knack; a contemptuous term for a person' (apparently from Gaelic *boch*, 'ecstasy, great happiness'), *coorag*, 'index finger' (< Gaelic *corrag*) and *buckie-failie*, 'the fruit or flower of the briar; the primrose', from Gaelic *bocaidh-fhàileag*, 'the hip, the fruit of the wild rose'. The intimacy of the contact between the two languages in this area can be seen in examples such as a sub-meaning for *sauf*, 'save' (originally borrowed from French), 'draw (a boat) up on the shore for the winter', apparently calquing a sub-meaning of Gaelic *gleidh*, 'preserve'.

The intimate nature of these contact can be seen in words like *hippans*, 'hips, the fruit of the wild rose', where the diminutive form of this originally English word (*hips*) is Gaelic in origin.

Some of these borrowings, such as *slake*, 'one of various species of edible fresh- and salt-water algae', apparently from Gaelic *slòcan* (although Irish influence is also possible), are also to be found in the Northern Isles. These may have been borrowed from other Scots dialects or directly from Gaelic through contacts, whether ancient or recent, with the Western Isles or Ireland. With this particular example, the latter is made likely by its presence in Faeroese, as *slavak*, since the Gaelic influence on those North Atlantic North Germanic varieties which were not ruled from Scotland would, at least in every likelihood, have dated from the early to high middle ages, when the Western Isles of Scotland and parts of Ireland were ruled by Scandinavians and there were significant levels of Scandinavian settlement.

It is illuminating that, again, so many of these words and phrases are connected with the formerly prevalent way of life. Because of the long-term nature of the contact between Gaelic and Scots on the northern mainland, as discussed further in Chapter 5, these Gaelic resources are among the central sources of the distinctiveness of Northern dialects. But because of their subject matter, they are under as much threat as other elements of the local variety.

4.6.2 *Scandinavian influence*

There is a considerable amount of Scandinavian lexis in all Scots dialects. Because it is a secondary contact dialect in relation to the large-scale Scandinavian settlement in northern England in the early Middle Ages (Samuels 1989), a large part of this lexical material – words which appear typically 'Scots', such as *brigg*, 'bridge', and *kirk*, 'church' – is shared with the dialects of northern England, however. But there are some Scots-speaking areas where primary contact took place, particularly the Northern Isles, but also Caithness. The different levels of Scandinavian influence felt by dialects of Scots and English can be illustrated in figure 4.2.

There are many examples of the primary contact in the Northern Isles. Words associated only with Shetland include *snug*, 'to strike, push, try to prod with the horns' (for which comparison could be made to Norwegian dialectal *snugga*, 'to push, shove'), or *ball*, 'to roll together; put in disorder', apparently from Old Norse *ballrast*, 'crowd together in a confused throng'. Words only attested for Orkney include *quink*, 'the brent goose or greylag goose', probably from Old Norse *kveinka*, 'to whine, whirl'. There also a number of words, such as *immer*, 'the great northern diver', derived from Norse, which are confined to the Northern Isles collectively.

A number of Scandinavian borrowings are attested only for Caithness, such as *leens*, 'pieces of grassy land in a moor or by a river, meadows, frequently pastures of natural grass', and *ingy*, '(of a ewe) give birth to (a lamb)', as well as some which are shared in common between that county

Figure 4.2 Levels of Scandinavian influence on Scots and English dialects. Full lines imply primary contact; broken lines imply secondary contact. The thicker the line, the more intense the contact was.

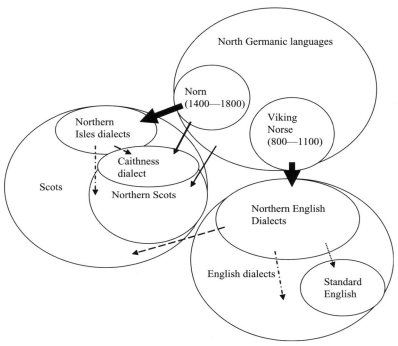

and the Northern Isles, such as *knotty*, referring either to the game of shinty or the ball used in the game, and *swelchie*, 'a whirlpool in the sea'.

What is striking, however, is that there is a considerable amount of lexical material borrowed from Norse which is not attested in the dialects of England, but nonetheless not confined to Shetland, Orkney and Caithness. These include *laggin*, 'the projection of the staves beyond the bottom of a barrel', and *meith*, 'boundary marker'.

Many of these examples – although by no means a majority – are largely attested for the northern regions of Scotland, whether including the Northern Isles, as with words such as *cair*, whose primary sense is 'stir', or *kav*, *kaif*, 'foam in breaking, throw up a spray'. Some include apparent idiom transfer, such as *ill-best*, 'the best of a bad lot', found throughout the Northern Isles and the northern mainland, which appears to be based on a Norse model. Some, such as *dag*, 'thin, drizzling rain', are attested only for the northern mainland (including Caithness), but not for the Northern Isles; others, such as *floan*, 'show affection, especially in a sloppy way', are attested only for the North-East, where primary contact with Scandinavian dialects, while not impossible through the North Sea and Baltic trade, was much less intense than it was further north.

What are we to make of such apparent anomalies? On occasion, with words such as *belch*, 'belly', associated in particular with south-west Scotland, primary contact with Norse speakers – perhaps from the Isle of Man – is possible, if unprovable (although this would almost inevitably imply transfer via the Gaelic dialects spoken in this area when Norse dialects were still used in places around the Irish Sea). With others, such as *lachter*, 'the total number of eggs laid by a fowl in a season; a single clutch on which she broods', the phonology – in particular the preservation of /x/ before /t/ – suggests a borrowing during the Viking period, when this sound was still present in this context in Scandinavian varieties; the word has probably been brought into what is now Scotland through secondary rather than primary contact.

The fact that many of these words are not attested for northern English dialects may give us pause for thought, but can be explained by the assumption that the word has ceased to be used in the primary contact area, but is still present elsewhere. This might be profitably compared with the survival of words and expressions in North American varieties of English, such as *Fall*, 'Autumn', previously common in England, but now only found in a few dialects. In some senses these survivals can be seen as examples of 'colonial lag' (as discussed in, for instance, Görlach 1987). It is also quite possible that the same word could be borrowed on two (or more) occasions: once in the Insular and Caithness primary contact zone and once through secondary contact with Scandinavian influenced northern English dialects.

With the examples of use of a form across the northern mainland, many of these possibilities are present. There are some examples, such as *cassie*, 'straw basket or pannier', which were originally confined to the Northern Isles, but were eventually spread throughout the North. This was probably common in the fisheries. Again, it is also possible that two discrete borrowings have taken place, with the naturally conservative northern mainland dialects using a form previously found all over Scotland due to secondary contact, while it has been borrowed directly in the primary contact zone. On occasion, it is quite likely that one process (or processes) has supported the other, reinforcing the use of a rare word.

The fact that we can talk in these terms about borrowings from the Scandinavian dialects emphasises how relatively closely related languages can interact in a domestic and low-key way, encouraging intimate borrowings. The semantic fields of most of the borrowed words – largely associated with everyday life – demonstrate this particularly forcefully.

4.7 Conclusion

This chapter has attempted to illustrate the lexical richness and diversity of the dialects of northern Scotland and the Northern Isles in comparison with the more southerly dialects of Scots. This richness and diversity can be derived from the fact that the region acts as a relict area for usage which in earlier varieties of Scots was much more widespread; part of this retention can be explained by the survival of traditional social patterns and occupations. Indeed, much of the distinctive lexis refers to these practices and occupations. Moreover, as is the case with mountainous regions of Norway, Italy or Afghanistan, the terrain encourages small-scale linguistic distinctiveness. Finally, the local dialects have come into more intense contact with other languages than other Scots varieties; this close contact has inevitably encouraged the local vocabulary to become significantly different from that found elsewhere.

This level of diversity should not be taken for granted, however, as the next chapter will demonstrate.

5 History, including changes in progress

5.1 Introduction: language contact and language shift

With sufficient perspective, the linguistic history of northern Scotland and the Northern Isles is one where, on a number of occasions, the inhabitants have changed languages, although what these languages were has differed from region to region. Therefore, to understand many of the distinctive features of these dialects, we need to understand how the inter-related phenomena of language contact and language shift work upon the variety speakers are shifting to.

Language shift has always happened. When we look at the Mediterranean basin today, we can see that many languages, such as Gaulish, Etruscan or Punic, whose speakers wielded considerable power, are no longer spoken. In their place are languages associated with political power and cultural uniformity, such as Latin and its Romance daughters or Turkish, languages associated with an all-pervasive ideology, such as Arabic, or languages associated with immigration, such as the Slavonic languages.

If these processes can be illustrated for areas with a lengthy recorded history, it would be perverse to suggest the opposite for areas less well reported, such as those discussed here.

Sasse (1992) provides a model for what happens when one language dies, and another takes its place. How does transfer from one language to another affect the language of the transferring community? How does it affect the language of those who speak the target language?

Three variables interact during the process of language shift (Sasse 1992: 10). The first is *external setting*: what features in the society, culture and history of both the speakers of the abandoned (A) language and of the target (T) language bring about the shift? Further, there is *speech behaviour*: in what contexts, and to which people, do speakers of A use either A or T? Finally, what are the *structural consequences* for both the A language and, in particular, the T language?

Figure 5.1 A model of language shift (from Sasse 1992: 19)

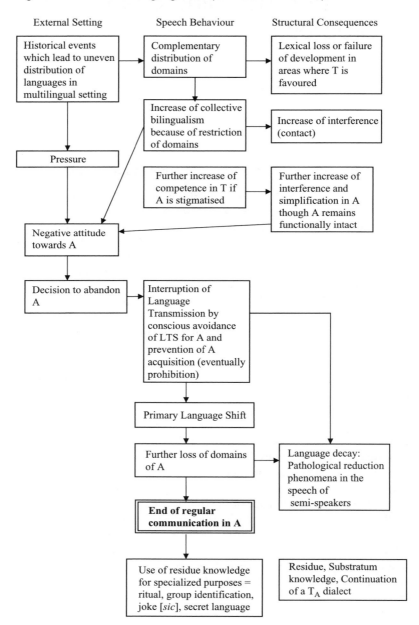

Terms and Definitions

A = *Abandoned Language* (Language which is dying out); *T* = *Target Language* (Dominant language which is continued); *Primary Language* = L with higher degree of lexical, grammatical and pragmatic competence; *Secondary Language* = L with lower degree of lexical, grammatical and pragmatic competence; *Language Replacement* (= Complete Shift) = Total replacement of A by T (possibly T_A, i.e. an A-influenced variety (dialect) of T); *Language Transmission* = Purposive, directed passing-on of a language from one generation to the next; *Language Transmission Strategies (LTS)* = The whole array of techniques, used by adults to assist their children in first language acquisition, e.g. 'motherese', repetitions, exercise games, corrections, metacommunication, etc.; *Language Decay* = Pathological language disintegration; *Semi-Speaker* = Member of the post-Language-Transmission break generation with imperfect knowledge of A; *Terminal Speaker* (Sometimes confused with imperfect speaker) = Last generation speaker; *Simplification* = Removal of linguistic complexities; *Reduction* = Removal of significant/essential/ functionally necessary parts of the language.
(Sasse 1992: 18)

Much of this is common sense. In an external setting where there is an 'uneven distribution of languages in [a] multilingual setting' in which particular contexts – *domains*, as they are often termed by sociolinguists – are reserved for the prestige variety, there will eventually be lexical loss or failure of development for the low-status language where the high-status language is considered the most suitable. More speakers of the disparaged variety will inevitably feel obliged to learn the prestige variety.

Equally inevitably, since these speakers will not gain absolutely 'perfect' command of the new variety, elements of their native language's structure will be carried over into the new language. Simultaneously, since the new language is spoken regularly and may well be admired by speakers of the disparaged variety as being more 'correct' than their native language, some elements of the new language's structure will be carried back into the native language.

As time goes on, the A-speaking population will become more competent in T, using it both in prestigious domains, and increasingly in the more domestic, family-centred, domains in which A was previously secure. Linguistically, A will come under ever greater influence from T, involving considerable 'simplification' of the structure of the language (in particular those features not shared by the languages). Nonetheless, A is still a functioning language, with a considerable number of native speakers.

The growing negative attitudes towards A mean that elements within the population will decide to abandon it and only use T. The most natural forms of language transfer – from parent to child – will suffer. Although decisions of this type are unlikely to be universal, many children will only pick up the language in rather more casual contacts with other children and adults. This variety cannot be recognised fully as a 'native language', and will contain several features in its structure which will be different – often due to interference from T.

Dorian (1981) demonstrated that, while many members of the final generation of Gaelic speakers in East Sutherland retained native speaker competence, some, particularly those who had not spoken it regularly for decades, and whose families may not have used it as their home language, understood the language without difficulty, but, when prompted to speak it, did so in ways which demonstrated that the primary grammatical structure they employed was their native English (or Scots) variety. She termed these 'semi-speakers'.

These semi-speaker varieties are usually frowned upon by full speakers. This will increase the animus against A, now perceived as 'corrupt', from within the native community. Eventually, primary language shift will occur, so that, when A is used at all, it will be as a block of 'residue knowledge for specialized purposes' (Sasse 1992: 19). Perhaps the former speech community had distinct cultural or religious practices encouraging the retention of certain core words or phrases. Equally possibly, the community may wish to maintain its group identity, and therefore, despite (or perhaps because of) its overt lack of prestige, A words and phrases are used to express this identity.

Because of the 'messy' nature of these final stages, and perhaps also because of the need to express in-group identity, there will be some residue of the former language in the new: T_A.

In the following sections, Sasse's model will be tested against the various language contact and shift phenomena which occurred in our area.

5.2 Northern Scotland

The first substantial reference by ancient geographers and historians to northern Scotland is in Tacitus' discussion of the pacification campaigns of his father-in-law Agricola in northern Britain. In the late summer or early autumn of 83 or 84 CE, he tells us, a battle was fought between some tens of thousands of Romans (and auxiliaries) and a larger number of *Caledonii*, led by Calgacus, at a place named *Mons Graupius*, 'Mount Graupius'. The Roman troops eventually overwhelmed the Caledonii, whose losses were immense.

Tacitus' description is problematical – not least because the totality of Roman victory is questionable, given that they did not follow up their success. Even the site of the battle is in some doubt, although the most likely candidate is around Bennachie, the easternmost of the Grampians, in the Garioch (Marren 1990: Chapter 1). Nonetheless, he presents us with some information on the inhabitants of the North at this time, their social structure and material culture. For instance, Calgacus' name, meaning 'swordsman', is Celtic in origin.

In the third century, the historian Eumenius refers to a people named the *Picti* as inhabiting the same area. He glosses *Picti* as 'painted people', which commentators have assumed to refer to their tradition of tattooing. This may be an example of folk etymology, however: the name, long obscure in meaning, was also used by the people to refer to themselves.

Early medieval Irish historians describe the new Gaelic colony in western Scotland as being involved in the affairs of its larger and more powerful eastern neighbour, a people termed *Cruithni*, etymologically equivalent to *Britons*, whom, we can assume, are the same people as the Picts. At the same time, the intrusion of Northumbrian power into the central lowlands of Scotland inevitably led to a clash between the Angles and the Picts, won by the latter at the battle of 'Nechtanesmere' (probably Dunnichen in Angus) in 685 (Fraser 2002).

As Wainwright (1955), Smyth (1984), Cummins (1995) and Dunbavin (1998) point out, the cultural artefacts of prehistoric northern Scotland portray a society where handicrafts had become impressively sophisticated. The defensive features associated so strongly with this part of Scotland, such as the *brochs*, suggest the presence of a widely dispersed rather than concentrated ruling class. Large-scale settlements appear to have been mainly unknown, although the Inverness area achieved some importance towards the end of prehistory (or, at least, semi-history). There is also considerable evidence for long-distance trading and herding.

Discussion of what kind of language Pictish was (if, indeed, it was one language) has provoked heated debate. The remaining inscriptions, in Roman and Ogam scripts, are both confused and confusing. Many scholars (particularly Jackson [1955]) have argued that, while some inscriptions are P-Celtic (a language more closely related to Welsh and Breton than Gaelic), others represent a language which was not Celtic, and may not have been Indo-European. Forsyth (1997) recently overturned this view, demonstrating that all the inscriptions are undoubtedly P-Celtic, a point reinforced by their Gaelic name *Cruithni*, discussed above.

The place name evidence largely supports this view. For while many of the river names of northern Scotland appear to be pre-Celtic

(Nicolaisen 1976), the names of many places, such as Kin*cardine* (cp. Welsh *cardden*, 'thicket') or Strath*peffer* (cp. Welsh *pefr*, 'shining') and, quite possibly, the *aber* in *Aber*deen (perhaps 'mouth of the Don'), include elements which are Celtic, but not Gaelic, even if Gaelic elements such as *kin* or *strath* have later been added to them. Indicative, perhaps, of difference between this variety of 'North British' and more southern dialects is the place name *pett*, 'place', so common in Scotland north of the Forth, found in *Pit*sligo, *Pitt*endreich, *Pit*skelly, and many others (Price 2000a).

Surprisingly, however, this language, spoken by the dominant Pictish part of the new Pict-Scot union of 843, was abandoned in favour of the language of the Scots, Gaelic. Why should this have happened? While some peoples cherish their language as a symbol of their identity, others do not, apparently perceiving language as a tool rather than a symbol, a point Fasold (1984: 17–19) exemplifies in modern times. Considerable numbers of Gaelic speakers (at least as evinced by their names in genealogies) moved into Pictland, bringing the new prestige language with them. Moreover, the association of Gaelic with Christianity should not be underestimated. By the time of the death of Macbeth (1057), the North-East in particular had become the heartland of Gaelic language and culture in Scotland.

5.2.1 North-East Scotland

As Shepherd (1987) and Ralston (1987) demonstrate, the apogee of Gaelic culture in the North-East was reached in the tenth to twelfth centuries, when works such as the *Book of Deer* were produced, suggesting a powerful Gaelic-based church (Jackson 1972). Unlike more westerly regions, there was little long-term disruption caused by Scandinavian invasion and settlement, meaning that this culture was able to expand and evolve independently.

Outside the church, most inhabitants were involved in subsistence-level agriculture and fishing. The name *Buchan*, 'cow place', is suggestive of the cattle rearing and herding associated with the area in later times. Much of the low-lying land which would later be cultivated systematically was left fallow, because of ineffective ploughs and drainage. There is considerable evidence, however, for greater cultivation in higher areas than would be considered profitable today. Something like the later clan system probably existed, with chieftains holding power – and property rights – associated with both territory and kinship.

Scotland was changing, however. Under the sons of Malcolm Canmore (reigned 1057–93) and St Margaret, the Gaelic character of the monarchy was discarded in favour of the prevailing views on religious, cultural and, in particular, political and economic structures emanating from France through Norman England. Development of a money-based economy and of long-distance trade was crucial. Because the nobility were considered a threat to central government, a new nobility based upon hierarchical feudalism, where all power and property emanated, in theory, from the king, was instituted. To do this, power and property had to be moved from the old nobility to the new, whether by violence or, often, the astute use of marriage and inheritance. This new nobility was composed largely of minor gentry of Norman or Flemish origin from northern England and the Welsh marches. The experience which these marcher lords had in maintaining 'order' in debatable lands must have been attractive to the king.

At the same time, the monarchy was gradually moving its power base south and east – from the Perth area to the south coast of Fife and, eventually, Lothian. As Macafee (2002) demonstrates, the South-East was the only part of Scotland in which Old English had been able to maintain its hold following the collapse of Northumbria as a result of the Scandinavian incursions. Lothian's Northumbrian dialect, combined with the northern English dialects which the followers of the Norman settlers brought with them, is the ancestor of all the modern Scots dialects.

Scots primarily spread through the establishment of *burghs*, originally fortified trading settlements and instruments of royal and noble control, at places of economic and strategic importance throughout the kingdom (although their presence was limited in the highland areas of the north and west). The Anglian dialects of the burghs must have been associated with the new order and prosperity; many inhabitants of their hinterland felt obliged to learn them in order to participate in the new economy. While burgh citizens probably learned enough Gaelic to trade, it is very likely that this was not established on an equal footing. In fact, a stable form of diglossia (Ferguson 1959), with Gaelic as the Low variety and the Anglian dialect as the High, must have existed in many places.

In the central lowlands, the transition from Gaelic to Scots was probably relatively painless, with Gaelic gradually retreating into the higher and more marginal areas, dying out completely in its last heartlands of Galloway and Fife by the eighteenth century. The situation in the North-East was more complex, however.

First, the relatively straightforward communication possible in southern Scotland was impossible north of the Grampians. Moreover, the loyalty of the North-East to the central monarchy was questionable. Finally, the possibility of greater prosperity through agriculture was hampered by limited technology. This meant that the burghs founded in this area were incapable of the geographical influence their southern equivalents had, except where, as with Aberdeen, communication with the south was possible by a low-level land crossing or by sea.

The burghs of the North-East did have some cultural and economic effects upon their hinterland. But outside those areas where arable farming was not only possible but also profitable – the lower lying areas of Mar, the Garioch and Moray – transhumance and subsistence farming remained the norm. The surplus necessary for the development of a market-based economy was in good years rather limited, and in bad years non-existent.

The ancient, clan-based, traditions and culture were maintained in the mountainous regions. Some originally Norman nobles appear to have 'gone native', behaving as if they were Gaelic chieftains rather than feudal lords. The most noteworthy of these were the Frasers, Gordons and Grants.

Unsurprisingly, therefore, it was in the coastal plains, in the hinterland of Aberdeen, Banff and Elgin, for instance, that local people first began to mimic the Scots speakers of the burghs. Of course this process was unlikely to be swift. Elsewhere (Millar 2004) I have suggested that the 'frontier' between one language and another probably did not often exist as a line on a map; rather, there would have been margins around all the more prosperous settlements and farms: margins inhabited by the lesser peasantry and farm servants. While the burghers and the larger farmers probably knew 'kitchen Gaelic', the language of prestige was Scots. As its use spread, the margins of everyday Gaelic use would retreat; the language may have taken centuries to disappear altogether, however.

The situation was different for Buchan, however, where the Bruce family's attacks on the estates of their enemies, collectively termed *the harrowing of Buchan* (1307 or 1308), marked the end of the high Gaelic culture in that region. Gaelic in Buchan, as elsewhere outside the mountains, became the language of a peasantry, their leaders speaking a different and more prestigious language.[1]

Throughout the medieval and early modern periods, the coastal parts of the region, in particular Aberdeen, took part in a wider North Sea and Baltic culture. Although connections were strong with Scandinavia, Hanseatic ports such as Danzig (Gdansk) and Lübeck in particular traded with Aberdeen; some Aberdonians moved temporarily or permanently to the Baltic region. During this period, many Dutch- or Low German-speaking immigrants moved into the burghs, often attracted by tax concessions offered because of their skills in weaving and other trades. In the seventeenth and eighteenth centuries Aberdeen also became home to numbers of French Protestant refugees. Again, these immigrants were particularly welcome because of their skilled backgrounds.[2]

While the descendants of these immigrants would probably not have spoken their ancestral languages by the fourth generation, the low populations of almost all the burghs except Aberdeen could well have made their presence more linguistically significant than in larger settlements.

A language variety probably developed which allowed increased intelligibility between speakers of these Germanic languages: Scots, Dutch, Low German and, perhaps, the Scandinavian dialects. Because of the 'founder principle' (Mufwene 2001: in particular, pp. 28–9), the greatest and most prestigious of these influences was Scots, and North-East Scots has very much remained a Scots dialect. We cannot discount interference phenomena in Low German or Dutch speakers using Scots. Mainly lexical, in words such as *loon*, 'boy, young man' or *haar*, 'cold summer fog', this influence possibly also explains the especially prevalent use of diminutives, a feature shared with the dialects of the northern Netherlands in particular.

Inland, however, the burghs were probably less effective as 'transmitters' for the new language than elsewhere in Scotland during the same period. Their remoteness from the main trading centres meant that, until the eighteenth century, their inhabitants would have lived not much higher above the subsistence level than their rural neighbours. If we take Inverurie as an example, illiteracy was practically universal in the burgh in the sixteenth and seventeenth centuries, even among its town council (Milne 1947). While there is no evidence of the burghs becoming Gaelic-dominant, it is likely that considerable knowledge of the language existed in at least the more up-country burghs such as Huntly, Keith or Rothes. This language contact, along with those caused by immigrant languages, encouraged a variety of Scots which was strikingly different from that of the lowlands.

Is there any evidence for this contact dialect? This is very difficult for the first few hundred years of the 'plantation' of Scots in the North-East. Barbour's *Brus*, for instance, written in Aberdeen during the fourteenth century, shows few or no North-Eastern features. Nor do the early records of the corporations of Aberdeen and other burghs or letters written by people from the area. In the sixteenth and seventeenth centuries, there are, however, occasional spellings which suggest Northern features, often in more intimate written contexts such as diaries or commonplace books. This is in accord with Macafee's observation (1989: 432) that local dialects 'must already have diverged significantly from Central Scots even in the Middle Scots period', as exemplified by McClure (2002: 22).

It should be noted, however, that writing is not speech. It is relatively straightforward to write using one register or dialect with a spelling system which reflects a particular pronunciation, while at the same time speaking a completely different dialect whose pronunciation cannot really be represented by the same spelling system. Indeed, the occasional 'northernisms' mentioned above might represent this phenomenon, with scribes attempting to use the standard variety's lexis and orthography, but occasionally using local spellings.

Second, we have no evidence to suggest that Barbour, or any other North-Eastern writers of the period, actually spent their linguistically formative years there, even if, particularly with materials composed by the local gentry, this would at least occasionally have been the case.

It is possible to envisage a situation where a form of diglossia existed between a more mainstream form of Scots, used by the gentry and civic officials, associated with the written form, and a local spoken variety which had maintained a great deal of its original material from the imported Scots, but where a few features (some lexical items, the merger of original /f/ and the local realisation of <wh>, possibly the lack of expressly plural forms for the demonstrative pronouns) had been caused by casual contact between different languages in the burghs and their hinterland. That is not to say, of course, that many of these features, for instance plural *that* and *this*, were not available within the wider pattern of variation of English during this period, as Macafee and Ó Baoill (1997) point out; merely that their reinforcement was encouraged when many, mostly non-literate, speakers were not certain of the 'correct' usage.

The relatively high proportion and varied semantic fields of the lexical borrowings from Gaelic into the Scots of this area, as discussed in Chapter 4, must also be borne in mind. Unusually for Scots as a whole, these patterns provide evidence for lengthy and intimate contact between the two languages in everyday communication.

Evidence is sparse, however. Given the environment in which I have proposed the creation of the contact dialect, written evidence is inevitably difficult to find; there are some tantalising hints, however. One of these is an early seventeenth-century letter purportedly sent home by an indentured servant in Maryland, Donald McPherson, to his father, James, in Culloden (near Inverness), written for him by one James Macheyne, originally from Petty in Aberdeenshire. The letter may not be entirely authentic, particularly since no original manuscript exists. The language and some of the subject matter are impenetrable enough, however, to raise the suspicion that the language at least is a fair representation of someone's speech. Millar (1996: 404–6) discusses these matters more fully.

The language of Donald's letter could only have come from the North-East. There are examples, for instance, of /ʍ/ becoming /f/, as in

> for de *fyt Fowk* dinna ise te work pat te first yeer aftir dey kum in te de Quintry, 'for the white people do not have to work except for the first year(s) after they come into the country'

This example also contains an example of a /w/ glide after a velar plosive in *Quintry*. Moreover, there is an example of /wr/ becoming /vr/ in

> Luck dat yu duina forket te **vryt** til mi ay, fan yu ket ony Ocashion, 'Look that you don't forget to write to me always, when you get any occasion'.

With the vowels, there are also plentiful examples of typically North-East features, such as the characteristic /i/ in *seener*:

> I wis I hat kum our hier twa or trie yiers **seener** nor I dit, 'I wish I had come over here two or three years sooner than I did'.

Although there are also a few features in the letter which are either English or more mainstream Scots, we can probably explain most of them as either spelling conventions or errors brought about by transcription.

There is another linguistic presence in the letter, however. The confusion of voiced and unvoiced consonants, as seen in

> **Pi** mi fait I kanna komplin, 'By my faith I can't complain',

as well as confusion between /s/ and /ʃ/, as in

> I **wis** I hat kum our hier twa or trie yiers seener nor I dit

and a lack of /ð/ and /θ/, as in

> Got Almichte pliss yu Fater an a **de** leve o **de** hous, 'God Almighty please you, father, and all the rest of the house'

or

> I wad a bine ill leart gin I had na latten yu ken **tis**, 'I would have been badly brought up if I hadn't let you know this'

would not be normal in contemporary North-East Scots. They are, however, consistent with features found in the English of native speakers of Gaelic (and sometimes, as with Caithness, the Scots of the descendants of Gaelic speakers, as discussed in Chapter 2). Of course we cannot build a solid argument upon the witness of one document; nonetheless, we can speculate on its implications.

First, it provides evidence for where Gaelic was spoken in the North-East during this period. General surveys such as Withers (1984) have tended to suggest that, by the eighteenth century, Gaelic was not spoken in the North-East except in the mountainous west including upper Deeside and Donside, but not the agricultural area around Petty. Donald's letter suggests that Gaelic-speaking individuals were still found in the lowlands of the Garioch and the Formartine at that time. As I suggested above, the poorest of farm servants and cottars probably kept their Gaelic in home and family contexts for a considerable period.

Returning to Sasse's model, the variety hinted at in the letter appears to be a particularly good example of T_A, a target-language dialect exhibiting some transference phenomena from the abandoned language. Because of the length of the contact envisaged, as well as the low status of the abandoned language, the greatest interference is to the phonology rather than the lexis or syntax. We must also remember that Macheyne was literate in English and had lived in an English-speaking area for a considerable period before he wrote this letter.

But no variety with all the phonological features of Donald's letter is spoken in the North-East today. To understand what happened to the class of people who might have spoken in this way, we have to understand the great changes in agriculture, education and social structure which affected the area from the late eighteenth century on.

Moving in a wave from the central lowlands, farming methods in Scotland changed from one largely dependent upon small-scale subsistence peasant agriculture to one which encouraged large farms run according to rational, scientific and capitalist methods (Campbell 1985; Devine 1995: Chapters 7 and 8). Deriving many of its insights from the Enlightenment, this movement for *improvement* had profound effects on the lives of most Scots, for good and ill.

In the North-East, *improvement* meant the development of field drains sufficiently well made that all but the marshiest low-lying areas could now be brought into cultivation. The larger farms implied that agricultural technology, generally beyond the means of small tenant farmers, could now be brought to bear; it also meant that, instead of working their own small plots, poorer country people were either compelled to move into the developing urban and industrial areas or became agricultural labourers.

New strains of larger and healthier animals were introduced, with many larger farms on the Buchan plateau abandoning arable farming altogether. With the advent of canals and, especially, railways, the rural North-East became readily accessible for the first time.

Thus developed a form of life peculiarly associated with the culture of the North-East, although similar forms of rural employment were found elsewhere in Scotland (Anthony 1997). Agricultural labourers were generally not permanently employed by one farmer; instead, unmarried servants in particular were employed for either a quarter- or a half-year, after which they could be hired by the employer who offered the best pay and conditions at a *feein mairt*, the *fee* being the agreement sealed by *arles*, 'earnest money', between the master and servant. On *flittin day*, when servants moved from one employer to another, roads were often filled with people and carts. Although some servants went considerable distances for their new employment, most stayed within a relatively small area, generally dominated by a market town. This movement within a circumscribed region probably encouraged the homogeneity of the local dialect, at the same time encouraging its peculiarities in relation to other varieties.

Unmarried servants generally lived either in a *bothy*, a separate bunkhouse where they cooked the food provided by their master, or in a *chaamer*, a part of the main farmhouse, where their food was cooked by a *kitchie deem*. The farmer himself was often referred to as *Mains*, while the farm was run by a *grieve*. The *bothy* or *chaamer loons* developed over time a culture based upon the singing of long narrative ballads, often set to traditional airs, which were regularly satirical in nature and helped preserve many of the distinctive features of the local dialects. Married farm servants often lived in small cottages close to the main farmhouse.

This way of life continued well into living memory, when mechanisation made many of the tasks carried out by agricultural labourers redundant. Its distinctive language is discussed in Fenton (1987).

On the coasts, fishing developed through the use of larger vessels and by improved means of preservation. Deep-sea fishing at a considerable distance from the home port became possible through mechanisation; associated trades such as fish-gutting became increasingly industrialised. Fishing communities were particularly strongly networked, with ties often closer to other fishing communities than with their hinterlands, a point illustrated for Shetland by Telford (1998). The fishers also regularly followed different religious traditions from the non-fishing inhabitants of their towns and villages. This may explain the often striking differences between fishing and farming varieties. Many of the local terms for the tools and experiences of the fishing trade, as well as peculiarities such as *tabu*-avoidance language (see Chapter 4) were perpetuated as local shibboleths.

Improvement also affected the position of Gaelic. Since the language – at least outside its mountainous heartland – was associated with the most marginal elements of the farming community, it is not surprising that *improvement* meant that most such labourers and subsistence peasant farmers were either forced off the land or included in the much wider – and Scots-speaking – *bothy/chaamer* culture. It is likely that estrangement from a specific ancestral base also encouraged a move away from the ancestral language.

In highlands districts, the most extreme form of *improvement* – clearance of land for sheep farming – also caused the break-up of Gaelic-speaking communities. By the end of the nineteenth century most Gaelic speakers were found in the most marginal land in occupations which were under threat from the spread of new technologies.

Moreover, the spread of mass education in English was particularly dangerous for the maintenance of a largely illiterate Gaelic. The barrier between Scots and English is highly permeable, and has become increasingly so in recent years. This is not the case with Gaelic. This distinctiveness means that the endless debate on the status and nature of Scots in relation to English can be avoided. But the survival of Scots words and structures as a covert element in 'Scottish English' is unlikely to be replicated for Gaelic. It is not surprising, therefore, by the early twentieth century, Gaelic speakers in the North-East were not passing on the language to their children. Although the last speaker of Deeside Gaelic did not die until 1982, the language had been moribund for decades.

Scots, on the other hand, thrived, albeit in a largely diglossic relationship with written English. The lack of large-scale industrialisation meant that the urban dialects spoken elsewhere in Scotland – most notably in Dundee, Edinburgh and Glasgow – were slow to develop, even in Aberdeen. Although, eventually, an urban vernacular, *Toonser spik*, appeared, this was at a surprisingly late date, perhaps even since the Second World War. Elsewhere, traditional employment, the retarded development of an urban class system, along with the fact that emigration outpaced immigration, meant that local varieties were generally spoken by most of the community, no matter their occupation, although many also had command of Standard English.

In the course of the twentieth century, the North-East variety became known as *The Doric*, a term previously applied to all Scots varieties. This singling out may well have been due to this survival across the community, as well as its obvious distinctiveness in relation to more southerly dialects. Macafee (1997: 546) comments:

It seems likely that broad Scots will survive only in communities that have some degree of immunity to hegemonic external forces, which usually means rural communities with sufficient economic resources to prevent massive migration of the younger generation and sufficient self-assurance to absorb and nativise incomers. The north-east, Orkney and Shetland are the places that best fulfil these criteria. A particular characteristic of these areas is the vertical integration of the community. Middle-class people, including teachers, who have grown up in the area speaking the local dialect and participating in the local culture, are able to provide children with role models, demonstrating by example that local people can succeed, and that they can be bidialectal.

Recent research suggests that this may no longer be the case, however.

McGarrity (1998) noted that the *Toonser* variety of Aberdeen is disparaged, often by its own speakers, and often in relation to the rural varieties:

> . . . respondents identify with the quintessential Doric but are not interested in being associated with the urban variety. (McGarrity 1998: 147)

At least in terms of traditional lexis, the urban dialect of Aberdeen is much less 'dense' than it was in the past, or traditional rural varieties are today. This supports findings from elsewhere in industrial and post-industrial Scotland, as discussed by Macafee (1994) and Pollner (1985).

Naturally, Aberdeen dialect is not always perceived as bearing low prestige. As Macaulay (2005) demonstrates, working class speakers are often highly skilled in – and proud of– their local variety. Yet these abilities are not being passed on. McGarrity (1998: 162) reports that

> . . . respondents [are] torn between vernacular sentiment and educational aspirations for their children.

This resonates with some of the findings in Imamura (2004), where the considerable interest which schoolteachers have in promoting and using Scots in the classroom is often at variance with their views on what constitutes a 'good' Scots variety, largely associated with a hankering for a past culture with heritage connections.

This change is also observable in country districts. Hendry (1997: 82) suggests – with considerable justification – that there has been a breakdown in transfer of Scots in its densest lexical form from parents to children.

These findings are echoed in Middleton (2001), where knowledge of lexical items and, in particular, characteristic local phonological features, such as the additional of a labial glide in the equivalent of English *good*, were practically unknown among children on Deeside; indeed, what was known was generally a highly circumscribed set of stereotypical local features, such as /f/ for <wh>, combined with a number of urban Mid-Scots features. Tellingly, Scots no longer appears to be the language of the playground. Further evidence for many of these features can be found in Löw-Wiebach (2005).

Although reports of this type are relatively common throughout Scotland, what is striking about this change is that it is relatively rapid. While other factors – such as the globalisation of mass communication – are certainly important for our understanding of these changes, a particular feature, which it does not share with any other mainland area of Scotland, is the importance Aberdeen has had in the exploitation of North Sea oil.

From the initial discovery of oil in the North Sea from the 1960s on, and its rapid exploitation in the 1970s, the North-East has undergone considerable social change. In the first place, the presence of a number of large oil companies in Aberdeen has led to an influx of generally well-heeled immigrants who, characteristically, only settle in the city for a few years. This has often meant that both they, and their children, have either been unwilling or unable to create network ties within local communities, including assimilation towards the local variety. In wealthy areas both in the city and on Deeside in particular, incomers have often outnumbered locals, in particular in schools.

Relations between longer-term residents and locals have, on occasion, been strained, with the former being accused of driving house prices up and wanting to 'take over'. This has reached the point where 'interlowpers' have been described as 'white settlers', a term with resonances in the history of British imperialism (Jedrej and Nuttall 1996). In fact, traditional Scots is most readily visible in those areas – such as Moray, Angus and northern Buchan – where travel into Aberdeen is not easy.

At the same time, many working-class immigrants from the declining industrial areas of the Central Belt moved into the less affluent neighbourhoods; their more southerly dialect has had considerable influence on the pronunciation of *toonser spik* in particular. A good example of this is the use for the last twenty years or so of a highly fronted allophone of /u/ in the working-class speech of north Aberdeen, when dialectological studies were demonstrating that this pronunciation was only to be found in Angus and, in particular, the Central Belt. This suggests that the pronunciation has 'jumped' from urban centre to urban centre, before fanning out into the hinterland.

At the same time as the oil business was becoming central to the economy of the North-East, the traditional occupations – in particular fishing, but also farming – were in perhaps even terminal decline. Advances in farm technology meant that the skills possessed by agricultural labourers were no longer needed; the rapid depletion of fish stocks in the North Sea, along with the protectionism embraced by countries like Iceland, led to the drastic downsizing of the fishing fleet. Although the oil trade 'saved' Aberdeen economicically, formerly prosperous fishing ports such as Peterhead and Fraserburgh, along with smaller villages such as Buckie, Cullen and Gourdon, now suffer from out-migration and, in those areas which were within easy commuting distance from Aberdeen, gentrification.

Since so much of the 'flavour' of the local dialect was caught up in the vocabulary of these trades, as Downie (1983) demonstrates, much has inevitably been lost in the transition. Old local vocabulary has not been replaced with new local terms. Since the language has such an association with these past occupations, there has been an inevitable 'heritigi-sation': children are encouraged to learn poetry and songs from the past. Knowledge and, in particular, use of the language is in danger of being compartmentalised, however, with Scots no longer being the default code, but rather one brought out for special occasions.

Moreover, what remains of the local dialect is often confined to a small number of stereotypical phrases. In my own experience, I have rarely heard /f/ for <wh> with anything other than interrogative pronouns in the speech of anyone under the age of sixty, even in rural districts. Indeed, the stereotypical greeting *Fit like?*, 'how are you?', is one often heard even in the speech of recent incomers (as is the stereotypical response, *Jist tyaavin awaa*, 'just getting by').

Developments of this type can also be found outside the lexis and phonology of the North-East. In her work on the plural forms of demonstrative pronouns in the lower Garioch, McRae (2000 and 2004) has demonstrated that there is an ongoing shift from the use of plural *this* and *that* to the use of the Standard English forms *these* and *those* or, with the latter, non-standard *them*. This development appears to work along an age gradient, with the oldest speakers using hardly any standard forms in their speech, while many children of school age use few local forms. Perhaps because it is the less common form, plural *this* has been most affected by this change; indeed, a new form, *ese*, formed according to local phonological rules from *these*, appears to be replacing it. Plural *that*, on the other hand, has been retained in the speech of younger locals rather more, to the extent that it might be seen as another local identity stereotype.

But while some features have become markers of local identity, many of the changes which are at present affecting the area, such as the spread of glottalisation (Marshall 2003) and more fronted allophones of /u/ seem to represent the adoption of features associated with much larger linguistic units. The future of the Doric as a highly distinctive dialect is by no means assured.

Many of the points made for the North-East also hold true for the other areas where Scots is spoken in northern Scotland, with the proviso that, patchy though our knowledge is for the former area, the rest of the north is even less well-covered. Moreover, the recent history of the rest of the north of mainland Scotland, while sharing the decline of traditional work patterns, has not been affected to the same extent by the exploitation of oil resources.

5.2.2 Black Isle

As the contributors to Omand (1984) demonstrate, the importance of the position of Cromarty, Avoch and (to some extent) Fortrose on the Black Isle and the consequences of that position for defence and seaborne transport is central to our understanding of the linguistic history of their Scots-speaking inhabitants. All of these factors led to close connections between these communities and the southern coast of the Moray Firth. Many of these features are also present in the linguistic history of other burghs in the region; most notably, Dingwall and Dornoch.

From the late medieval period on, these settlements were Scots-speaking enclaves in a largely Gaelic-speaking region (Mowat 1981: 136). As with the North-East bilingualism was widespread. Nevertheless, town and country appear to have kept themselves separate, except during those periods, such as the late eighteenth and nineteenth centuries, where the highland clearances forced a great many Gaelic-speakers to become (at least temporary) residents of Cromarty (ibid.: 136; Ash 1991: 61). *Improvement* also brought some southern farmers into the area from the eighteenth century on (Mowat 1981: 136). It is likely that something like the language-based class system described by Dorian (1981), where those lower down the social scale being more likely to speak and use Gaelic, developed. Elderly residents of the Scots-speaking areas remember a variety of Scots used by *fishers* which was different from that of the *toonsers*, those who made their living from trade and manufacturing on land, however.

In the course of the nineteenth and twentieth centuries, the fishing trade declined. Moreover, the importance of the communities as ferry crossings gradually declined as better roads were built which avoided the Black Isle entirely. Eventually, the Beauly, Cromarty and Dornoch Firths were bridged. While the southern shore of the Black Isle was served by a railway, Cromarty was never connected to this network. At the same time, however, a major naval base with ship-repair facilities was established at Invergordon. After the decline of Britain as a naval power, these berths were used to refit oil rigs. While Cromarty certainly took part in these developments, the primary concern of the eastern Black Isle was a combination of farming and tourism. In the late twentieth century, many Black Isle communities became mainly dormitory settlements for workers in Inverness. One linguistic consequence of this, along with the death of Gaelic on the peninsula, appears to be the gradual replacement of Scots – in particular its characteristic lexis – by Highland English.

5.2.3 Caithness

As the contributors to Omand (1989) demonstrate, Caithness has for long acted as a crossing-place from the Scottish mainland to the Northern Isles and also from the Gaelic- (and Scots-) speaking communities into the Norse. Beyond archaeological evidence, much of what we know about the early development of the area is found in Norse literary works, especially the *Orkneyinga Saga*. It is not surprising, therefore, that the Norse aspect of Caithness history is much more easily researched than the Gaelic. The coastal strip of the county, as well as the 'triangle' between Latheron, John o' Groats and just west of Thurso, is dominated by Norse place names. The rest of the county, however, is associated with Gaelic place names. Small pockets of Gaelic names exist even in the most Norse areas (Nicolaisen 1982). Even more than the North-East, the Gaelic heritage of Caithness should not be ignored.

Whenever Norse died out in the area, it is likely that it was replaced in its heartland not by Gaelic but Scots. The distance between this abandoned language and the target one is not great even today, and would have been considerably less at the time. Wick, like other burghs elsewhere in Scotland, no doubt served as a point of influence for the spread of Scots in the county; it is very likely, however, that the burgh and associated settlements were already 'foreign' to the inhabitants of the inland areas.

Gaelic remained in its south-west heartland until very recent times, however, and seems to have had considerable effects upon the local Scots dialect, both in terms of the intonation patterns and some phonological elements, such as the confusion of /tʃ/ and /ʃ/ and, possibly, the over-correcting replacement (due to the lack of a voiced/voiceless distinction in most varieties of Scottish Gaelic) of /t/ by /d/ in word final position, along with the prevalence of back /l/ realisations and of a 'rolled' /r/. Caithness dialect is therefore much more certainly a T_A variety than North-East Scots.

Like the North-East, but unlike the Black Isle, Caithness speakers frequently have /f/ pronunciations for <wh> words. Whether this is a local Gaelic-influenced feature, or one borrowed from the North-East, is impossible to say.

Although in general Caithness dialect fits the model of being relatively conservative in comparison with the Scots of the Central Belt, it is nonetheless striking that a number of phonological developments in Scots as a whole – perhaps most notably the more front pronunciations of /u/ were, at least until relatively recently, considerably more prevalent than they were in the North-East. This may suggest that Caithness is a centre of independent phonological innovation.

Until well into the nineteenth century, Caithness remained among the most backward agricultural areas of mainland Scotland. Although rational farming methods, coupled with the encouragement of more scientific fishing in Thurso and Wick and the development of quarrying as a major employer, can be seen as part of the *improvement* programme, the county's precarious communication with the rest of Scotland meant that it was less influenced by its more southerly neighbours. Nevertheless, ports such as Thurso and Wick participated fully in both the fishing and whaling trades and therefore became rather more cosmopolitan, at least at certain times of the year, than their geographical position might suggest.

As was the case elsewhere in Scotland, traditional industries declined during the twentieth century, encouraging the already considerable out-migration. The county increasingly relied on tourism and through-traffic to Orkney. During the same period, rural depopulation meant that, by the middle of the century, Gaelic was practically moribund. From the 1950s on, Thurso was influenced by the establishment of the Dounreay experimental nuclear reactor some distance to its west along the north coast. This pumped considerable amounts of money into various parts of the local economy; it also meant that considerable numbers of technicians and their families – often termed *atomics* by the locals – moved to the area. Many Wick people in particular believe that Thurso speech has been made less Caithness by these developments.

Wick in particular has suffered from the decline of fishing. Unemployment is high; this has been exacerbated in recent years by the closure of Caithness Glass, the other main employer in the area.

Caithness has not been well-served by scholarly investigation of its dialect. The only general discussion is a brief one by Mather (1978), which has a considerable slant towards phonology. Wickens (1980, 1981) suggests that, at the time her research was being carried out, there was considerable understanding of local words among younger elements of the population. On the other hand, many of the terms associated with the formerly dominant occupations, such as fishing, appeared to be fading. Richard (2003) demonstrated that local lexis, along with many local pronunciation features, is maintained in general use by children in Wick. Black (2003) showed that the use of *this* and *that* as plurals was still considerable for all ages in Thurso, although *this* plural did appear to be less prevalent in the speech of younger informants. This suggests that the gradual replacement of local with standard or colloquial features, ongoing in the North-East, is only beginning in Caithness.

5.3 The Northern Isles

Despite their position on the edge of the European continental shelf, the Northern Isles bear witness to human settlement going back millennia. Many of the monuments associated with these early settlers are among the oldest known of their type in northern Europe; they already demonstrate considerable sophistication. But what language(s) the first settlers spoke is unknown and unknowable.

There is considerable place name evidence for Orkney, and some for Shetland, for speakers of a P-Celtic language living there before the coming of the Vikings. The presence of these 'Picts' is also noted by later Norse commentators. When the Norse arrived, monastic settlements were to be found on some smaller islands. They named the monks *papar*, a practice underscored by the presence of islands which have *Papa* or *Pappay* (and variants thereof) in their names. These monks were probably of Irish or Gaelic Scottish origin; communities of these monks were also found in the Faeroe Islands.

While it is likely that the arrival of heathens made at least most of the monks leave, the Pictish population must largely have remained, gradually intermingling with their new Scandinavian neighbours. It has been suggested (Schei 1988: 31) that the place name element *Petta*, Old Norse for 'belonging to the Picts', in a number of now deserted and marginal areas in Shetland, demonstrates the social position of Picts in the new Norse order.

Although the language of the original population must have been spoken for a considerable period, the language of the newcomers, associated with political and economic power, became the main language of use by the time regular written records began to be kept.

Where these newcomers came from is also a matter of conjecture, although what records survive of later Norn suggest relatively close connections both with the dialects of western and south-western Norway and the dialects of the Faeroes and Iceland (Barnes 1998: 13–16). Lexical evidence points, again, to the dialects of western and south-western Norway as having the most correspondences with the Norse element of the Scots of Shetland (Jakobsen 1932: I, xxxi–xxxvi). Most of the settlers probably came from this area, although people from other Norse backgrounds – in particular, Icelanders and Norwegians – visited and occasionally settled in the Northern Isles during their fully Scandinavian period.

When the Scandinavians began to settle in the Northern Isles is a matter of conjecture. Given that Shetland is considerably closer to Norway than either the Faeroes or Orkney, it would seem likely that they came there first. It was Orkney which became the greater power, however. Kirkwall became the heart of a centre of Scandinavian power during its period of expansion. Indeed, the Earldom of Orkney became a major player in the politics of the North Atlantic world, the earls being able to exert influence over events in the Western Isles, Man and Dublin, as well as in the western parts of Norway itself. Shetland was something of an appendage to Orkney during this period: indeed, it is only mentioned very occasionally in the *Orkneyinga Saga.*

This saga, although composed in Iceland, demonstrates an intimate knowledge of Orkney, describing the deeds of the ruling house over some 200 years, revealing the considerable dissent between factions of the family and their supporters on the islands, Caithness and Norway, often resulting in bloody, albeit brief, outbreaks of violence. The kings of Norway naturally distrusted their powerful subordinates; it was often in the king's interest to stir up dissent in Orkney in order to retard the Earldom's strength and influence. Indeed, eventually the leading families of the Northern Isles over-reached themselves, attempting a *coup d'État* in western Norway in 1193. After its failure, Shetland was removed from Orcadian rule. Instead it was either administered separately or along with the Faeroes; its inhabitants certainly maintained much closer ties with Norway than did the Orcadians (Schei 1988: 37).

In the period which followed, the kingdom of Norway declined. It was united with Denmark in the person of Queen Margaret, a union made more institutional (and also expanded in a rather shaky union with

Sweden) by the treaty of Kalmar in 1396. With the royal administration moving from Bergen to Oslo and, eventually, Copenhagen, interest in the North Atlantic colonies inevitably lessened. Eventually, both Orkney (in 1468) and Shetland (in 1469) were mortgaged to the Scottish crown. Although strictly speaking these archipelagos remained part of Denmark-Norway until the seventeenth century, the Scottish authorities treated the territories almost from the beginning as if they were fully Scottish, introducing a Calvinist form of Protestantism at the time of the Reformation, rather than the Lutheranism favoured in other Scandinavian territories, and ignoring the Norse common law of the islands.

The history of the Scandinavian dialects spoken in these parts of the North Atlantic is generally a matter of decline and death. We can set up a model whereby Norn – as it was called by some speakers and most scholars – 'retreated' into those colonies where Scandinavian rule was maintained: the Faeroes and Iceland. In Caithness and the Northern Isles, Norn died due to the pressure caused by the transfer of rule to, and penetrating influence from, the power centres of mainland Scotland. Thus Caithness Norn succumbed first, then Orkney Norn and finally the Norn of Shetland.

Later lexical evidence, as well as knowledge of the region's earlier history, suggests that for a considerable period a dialect of Norn was spoken in Caithness. Thorsen (1954: 234) suggests that

> While, therefore, Norn was extinct in Caithness in the middle of the seventeenth century, it may well, on the other hand, have outlasted the fifteenth. It should be remembered that throughout the sixteenth century the Orkney Norn was still vigorous and fit to support the sister dialect in Caithness.

This may well be the case; there is, unfortunately, little or no written evidence to support it. As we saw in Chapter 4, nonetheless, a very real Scandinavian 'flavour' is present in the contemporary dialect.

The fact that we know little or nothing about the decline of Orkney Norn may itself be significant. Even before the end of Scandinavian rule in the Northern Isles, the Earldom had passed to the Sinclairs, a Caithness family, in 1379. Inevitably this meant that the orientation of the Earldom shifted to the south. As Graham (1993: xiii) and Barnes (1984: 355) point out, the spoken Scots of the ruling house, the hand-over of land to the followers of the new earls and the presence of Scots-speaking merchants and clerks in Kirkwall would of necessity have attracted considerable prestige to Scots among the leaders of the native Norse community. This is reflected by the fact that, as Barnes (1984: 384) observes, 'the native Lawman of Orkney using the new language on internal Orcadian business' while the Northern Isles were still officially ruled from Scandinavia.

Given the proximity of Orkney to the Scottish mainland and the importance of Kirkwall economically and politically, it is likely that this Scots influence spread rapidly into all sections of the community. Barnes (1984: 355) observes that

> After the Reformation Scots (and English) gradually became the medium of religion. [Moreover] [c]onsiderable numbers of Scotsmen (apparently chiefly lowlanders from Angus, Fife and the Lothians) began to settle in the islands after 1400 (although immigration into Shetland was in general later and less intense).

Nevertheless, as Flom (1928–9: 148) points out,

> Mathew Mackaille, of Aberdeen, writes in the last half of the seventeenth century, in *A Short Relation of the Most Considerable Things in Orkney*. 'It is very probable that the inhabitants of the Orcades of old had only Noords, or rude Danish; but now there are only three or four parishes (especially upon the Mainland or Pomona) wherein that language is spoken, and that chiefly when they are at their own houses; but all speak the Scots language as the rest of the commons do' . . . As late as the last half of the XVIIth century, there were those in several places in Mainland, Orkney, who spoke Norse, when among themselves. And Rev. John Brand wrote, in 1701, in his *Description of Orkney and Shetland*, that Norse was not extinct yet in Orkney, 'though there be far more of it in Zetland [ie, Shetland]'.

The social situation of these last speakers of Orkney Norn is striking, and is in accord with the theory and experience of language shift observed elsewhere. As Fishman (1991 and 2001 in particular) has noted, and as we have already seen in Sasse's model of language shift, the gradual exclusion of a language from all but domestic contexts can lead to terminal decline for that language, particularly if another language is available and known by all, and is affecting inter-generational transfer of the home language. Moreover, the prestige which the Target language had would inevitably affect the position of the native variety, again discouraging and disrupting the transfer of that language by the most natural means.

The geographical position of the pockets of Norn on the Mainland of Orkney is also interesting, since the islands were dominated by the sea. The central area of that island was therefore cut off from the economic changes affecting the archipelago. Moreover, the agriculture which the inland parishes practised in the late seventeenth century would soon become obsolete due to *improvement*. When occupational culture is dissipated, the language associated with it often passes away as well, as Dorian (1981) suggests for the shift away from Gaelic in East Sutherland with the end of large-scale fishing. Significantly, while Gaelic and English are only distantly related to each other, Scots and Norn, although not mutually intelligible by this period, were close relatives with a considerable amount of central vocabulary in common, as Lorvik (2003) suggests in relation to the northern European timber trade.

If the Orkney Norn speakers had been able to maintain their cultural or religious identity as separate from the Scots incomers, their language might have been preserved for some time, as observed by Gal (1979) for the Magyar-speaking minority in eastern Austria. This was not possible, however, since Norse law was officially abolished in the Northern Isles as early as 1611 (Graham 1993: xiii) and the Protestant Reformation was carried out largely from the point of view of Scotland and an English Bible, although one of the last penetrable fragments of Norn recorded for Shetland is a version of 'The Lord's Prayer' which bears striking similarities to Scandinavian versions. Moreover, as we will see, the Church of Scotland took seriously its training of the ministry in 'Danish' when sending them to congregations in northern Shetland. Nevertheless, the cultural and economic pressures exerted upon Orkney Norn speakers to conform to Scots must have been considerable.

Relating this to Sasse's findings, the rather early shift of socially powerful speakers of Norn to Scots inevitably involved a stigma being attached to the former language as the language of the peasantry. Indeed, as we saw in Chapter 4, it was in contexts associated with fishing and crofting that Scandinavian borrowings into the Insular dialects of Scots were most prevalent. The fact that Scots had been spoken in Orkney for a lengthy period, as well as the presence of a nearby Scots-speaking area in coastal Caithness, may well explain why Orkney dialect seems less a T_A dialect than Shetlandic. It may also explain the 'singing' intonation of Orcadian speech, possibly derived from the Gaelic influence exerted upon Caithness Scots by Gaelic (van Leyden 2004).

Studying the death of Norn in Shetland involves somewhat less guess work, primarily because language shift occurred in many places in the islands in the eighteenth century when an antiquarian interest in local varieties had developed, and communications with Scotland were more straightforward than in the preceding centuries.

How early the shift took place depended, as with Orkney, on geography, although, since Shetland does not have a 'central plain' like the mainland of Orkney, this geographical distinction seems based on proximity to the southern parts of the Shetland mainland (Murison 1954: 255). In the northern isles, and in the more far-flung islands the language survived for much longer.

A distinction existed between the developing native middle classes and local people engaged in traditional pursuits. Lack of prestige for Norn would have encouraged this. In 1593, Magnus Manson, who had been appointed minister of Unst, had to be sent to Norway to learn his parishioners' native language (Flom 1928–9: 147; Murison 1954: 256). Manson possibly came from the southern end of the archipelago, but this still implies that language shift was nearly complete there.

During this crucial period, there appear to have been conflicting language attitudes present among the native population. To many, the new Scots/English language must have seemed to be the passport to a more prosperous future. This can be seen in the rhyme, possibly from around 1750 (Flom 1928–9: 155) 'said to belong to Unst' (Jakobsen 1897: 10):

De vaar e (vera) gooa tee,
'when' sona min 'guid to' Kaadanes:
haayn kaayn ca' *russa* 'mare,'
haayn kaayn ca' *bigg* 'bere'
haayn kaayn ca' *eld* 'fire'
haayn kaayn ca' klovandi 'taings'

'That was a good time, when my son went to Caithness: he can call *russa* "mare", he can call *bigg* "bere" [a from of barley], he can call *eld* "fire", he can call *klovandi* "taings" [tongs]' [my translation]. We are not immediately concerned with the structure of Norn as a language in itself, except insofar as it affects the form of the present Shetland dialect. Nevertheless, it is worth noting that, although elements of this rhyme represent authentic Norse grammatical structures, the central verb of a large part of it – <ca'> –is represented in its Scots form, rather than its Norse: with characteristic Scots vocalisation of /l/ and a lack of infinitive ending morphology (although this last feature is also present in a number of south-western Norwegian dialects).

On the other hand, evidence from the middle to late eighteenth-century demonstrates that the old folk culture and language of the islands were cherished by the local people. This can be seen, for instance, in the 'Hildina Ballad' (Hægstad 1900) taken down in 1774 by the Rev. George Low (who unfortunately knew no Scandinavian language) from the recital by an elderly farmer from Foula, William Henry, who claimed to have learned it as a child. As a number of commentators have pointed out (Flom 1928–9: 154–5; Barnes 1984: 356), the language of this relatively long poem appears to be authentically Norse, although with some evidence for reduction in morphological complexity. This is particularly impressive since Low reports that Henry did not understand the full meaning of the poem, instead giving a paraphrase of what he thought it meant. Low also recorded some phrases of Norn discussed at some length by Rendboe (1987).

The other useful fragments of Norn we have were recorded by Jakob Jakobsen during his fieldwork on Shetland in the 1890s. As a gifted linguist, and also a native speaker of Faeroese, his witness of what he heard is obviously considerably more trustworthy than that of Low. Jakobsen hints that Norn may have been spoken by a few people in the outlying isles in the middle of the nineteenth century. It is not entirely clear what he meant by Norn, however – perhaps a heavily Scandinavianised form of Scots; perhaps a fully functioning North Germanic variety – or even whether he was suggesting that Norn was still anyone's first language when his informants remembered it being spoken.

Barnes (1998: 21–31) presents three separate interpretations of how Scots replaced Norn. The first, associated with Jakobsen, Flom and Marwick, was that the Scots element in the Shetland dialect gradually swamped the Scandinavian; from this point of view, it is difficult to perceive the change in language. Over time, the originally Scandinavian structure of the dialect was altered by borrowing of structures from Scots (along with considerable amounts of lexis) to the extent that it becomes a dialect of Scots with Norse phonological and lexical residual features. Barnes discounts this view:

> . . . if for no other reason than that the imperceptible melting of one language into another they envisage seems to be without parallel. There is in addition the weakness that none of the three scholars argues a clear case for fusion; all the reader is offered is a series of inexplicit assumptions. Crucial terms such as 'Norn', 'Scots', 'dialect', 'language', etc. are used in a disconcertingly vague manner, to the extent that one is led to doubt whether the writers themselves always knew precisely what they had in mind. (Barnes 1998: 23)

While his points are well made, Barnes does not recognise that the contact which existed in Shetland was between quite closely related languages.

The second viewpoint Barnes discusses is that of Rendboe (1984 and 1987). Rendboe interprets the evidence to suggest a brutal takeover by

Scots speakers which was met with considerable resistance by the native Shetlanders. Using Jakobsen's hints about survival of Norn in some areas well into the nineteenth century, he makes a case for the 'purity' of the Norn recorded by Jakobsen in 1890s, as being used by people who had themselves heard – perhaps even used – Norn in their early years. As Barnes (1998: 23–4) puts it, '[while] it must be said Rendboe does his best to demonstrate the purity of Norn at different stages of its existence . . . the evidence he adduces can often be shown to point in precisely the opposite direction'.

The third interpretation which Barnes cites – the one he supports most – is that of Smith (1990 and 1996), who perceived the Shetlanders as, in the course of the seventeenth and early eighteenth centuries, losing their earlier multilingual and multicultural identity. In the early modern period, Shetland was the centre of a fishing and whaling enterprise involving speakers of Low German, Dutch, Scots, both insular and continental Scandinavian varieties, and Norn. As a result of the breakdown of this trade, the dominant – and hegemonic – language became Scots (in speech) and English (in writing). What followed, Barnes argues, was a normal language shift, with the perception among speakers of Norn that Scots (varying with English) was 'the language of the future', a view which eventually led to what Fishman terms the breach of intergenerational transfer of the mother tongue. Rejecting Rendboe's late date hypothesis for the death of Norn, Barnes (1998: 26) favours the end of the eighteenth century as when '. . . the last native speakers (those whose first language had been Norn) went to the grave'. This view has, in broad terms, been given support recently by Knooihuizen (2006).

While this sifting of the evidence does seem the most reasonable, it cannot be completely accepted. If Scots (varying with English) was so attractive during this crucial period, why is it that, some eighty or ninety years after Norn stopped being effectively anyone's mother tongue, Jakobsen could have recorded so much 'Norn', which was often very willingly and proudly offered?

Sasse's model of language death and its linguistic results is, again, helpful in these contexts. Certainly, there are elements of his analysis, such as 'increase of collective bilingualism because of restriction of domains', which seem in concord with Smith and Barnes' views on the language's decline. Another is 'negative attitude towards A'. To what extent can such negative attitudes be found in Shetland at the time? Of course we are, as ever, at the mercy of what has come down to us. Nevertheless, some evidence of such views can be found, at least from Rendboe's viewpoint, in the views expressed by middle-class commentators in the eighteenth century. But some of the surviving Norn fragments suggest, through the use of *skyimpin*, a lampooning of externally fashionable values frowned upon by the in-group (Schei 1988: 68), that the taking on of Scots values and language was not always popular. We could therefore claim that two competing language ideologies – one overt, the other covert, with the former dominant – existed in Shetland during the period.

Sasse also suggests that after the 'end of regular communication in A' there is 'use of residue knowledge for specialized purposes = ritual, group identification, joke [*sic*], secret language'. Might this not be what we have in the recording of Norn by both Low and Jakobsen? This seems to be connected by Sasse with 'residue, substratum knowledge, continuation of a T_A dialect' which, again, is likely to be what lies behind a great deal of the wordlist recorded by Low on Foula and discussed by Rendboe, rather than the entire survival of a language.

But why should this residue knowledge have survived so long in Shetland?

This 'half-life' of Norn might be explained by the shared lexis and (to some extent) structures of the source languages. As seen in the 'mixed' Caithness rhyme already cited, Scots and Norse have much in common with each other, exacerbated by the former's nature as a close secondary Norse contact dialect.

This, in its more potent Scots-Norn contact phenomenon role, could be seen as having a performative side to it – the 'ritual' aspect discussed by Sasse. A powerful expression of Shetland identity may be found in the use of half-understood, but well-remembered, phrases. It cannot be ruled out, in fact, that, even in the eighteenth century, some Shetlanders had learned to 'package' their culture, turn it into a heritage item for curious outsiders.

Further possible aids to partial survival can be found in the well-reported *tabu*-avoidance language of Shetland fishermen and, overwhelmingly, in the many similar cognate forms found in Norn and Scots, as discussed in Chapter 4. Thus Norn words and phrases were able to survive for considerably longer than might otherwise have been the case, influencing the new dialect in a manner reminiscent of a feedback loop.

The types of Scots brought into the Northern Isles were undoubtedly various – both in terms of the origin of the speakers and their position in society. Many scholars (for instance, Donaldson [1983: 12]) would point to the influence exerted by immigrants from both Fife and Angus; perhaps particularly the coastal burghs of Kirkcaldy and Dundee. Certain features of Shetland speech in particular – for instance the survival of front rounded vowels for the BUIT set – are possible relics of these contacts, since they are maintained in mainland Scots only in areas of rural Angus and Perthshire. While this association is tempting, it should be borne in mind that, at the time the contact was taking place, the rounded pronunciation was probably considerably more widespread, however.

Indeed, Barnes (1998: 28–9) argues that the survival of rounded front vowels in modern dialects is part of the Norn legacy. This does not, of course, rule out a double origin for the phoneme, with the Scots source reinforcing the Norn, and vice versa. The same can probably be assumed for the retention of *thoo* or *du* as a discrete second-person singular pronoun in the islands, although the rest of the paradigm (*dee*, for instance), is not Norn in origin.

Other scholars have also suggested further influences from Norn. Pavlenko (1997), for instance, has argued fairly convincingly that the use of *be*-perfectives with transitive verbs in the Shetland dialect, as discussed in Chapter 3, is, at the very least, a result of the interference between abandoned and target languages during the cross-over.

Undoubtedly, however, the greatest influence Norn has had upon the Scots of the Northern Isles is lexical. Although a number of scholars (most notably Jakobsen, Marwick and Graham) have charted the gradual loss of specifically Norn vocabulary in the Northern Isles, there is still much preserved in the dialect of Shetland in particular. Melchers (1981) demonstrated that the semantic fields associated with emotions, homely activities and flora and fauna were particularly well-represented in the dialect. This is supported by our findings in Chapter 4. Survival in these contexts is analogous with the semantic fields most resistant to change in most traditional dialects in highly literate countries. Elsewhere Melchers (1986) has demonstrated that the Scandinavian-based vocabulary of the islands has been subject to a considerable degree of semantic development, both in terms of narrowing and extension in meaning.

Too much can be made of the Scandinavian element in the traditional dialects of Orkney and Shetland, however, possibly because, in a post-Romantic Scotland, it is this feature, above all else, which expresses the difference between the Northern Isles and the Scottish mainland. In terms of the lexis of both dialects, much of the material is, or has been, shared with the more traditional mainland varieties.

There is some evidence, as suggested, for influence from East Central Scots on the Insular dialects, a point supported by lexical patterns shared with Angus, Fife and the Lothians, rather than the Northern dialects, as discussed in Chapter 4. This appears to be in line with the origins of many of the original mainland settlers. This point might be reinforced by the use of /no/ rather than /ne/ as a negator on the islands, although this is also true for Caithness.

It should be recognised, however, that many of the features of Insular Scots, not least the use of *this* and *that* as plural determiners and a large part of their non-Scandinavian vocabulary, are held in common with some or all of the Northern dialects. While some of this accord may be due to 'retreat' of previously common words, phrases and structures into areas where traditional lifestyles persisted until recently, close contacts between the two regions would seem the most likely explanation for most of these similarities.

To return to the historical record, it can be argued that the transfer of the Northern Isles from their North Atlantic world to one which was centred on the British Isles took a considerable period; indeed, it has never been completed. After the formal transfer of the islands in the late fifteenth century, many of the legal and governmental traditions of the old north were continued for at least a century. Nevertheless, over time, these old ways were supplanted by Scottish importations, as discussed in Donaldson (1983).

It would be wrong, however, to see the Northern Isles as peripheral in anything but a governmental sense. As already mentioned, Shetland thrived in the early modern period. Indeed, the islands' distance from the centres of power may have encouraged the development of fishing and whaling, since effective customs and excise provision was for a long period impossible, a point demonstrated in Friedland (1983), Boelmans Kranenburg (1983) and Smith (1984).

When a salt tax was imposed by the British government in the early eighteenth century, the 'boom' time was over; this did not mean, however, that the connections died out immediately. At the same time, the growing interest Britain had in what was to become Canada meant that Orkney became a stop-over point and victualling and watering station for expeditions in that direction. In the nineteenth century many Orcadians emigrated to Canada.

Indeed, emigration was particularly widespread throughout the Northern Isles during this period. Backward farming methods, coupled with the ravages of absentee landlords, meant that a continuation of the old way of life became increasingly infeasible. Subsistence-level crofting and fishing was the norm for most inhabitants. In Orkney in particular, the idea of 'getting on' by means of education was prevalent; many of the Orcadians who made their name in literary and other fields – Magnus Linklater and George Mackay Brown being among the most famous – came from relatively poor backgrounds where reading and learning were prized.

Although the old ties with long-distance trade and exploration dissipated, connections with the fisheries of the British Isles and the North

Atlantic were continued and, perhaps, intensified. In certain areas, most notably Scapa Flow in Orkney, the Royal Navy maintained a presence which became considerable during both World Wars. In the twentieth century – in particular as travel became swifter and more affordable – tourism joined farming and fishing as a major employer in the islands. The excellent raw materials produced particularly in Orkney were exploited in the manufacture of dairy products and whisky. Shetland – including Fair Isle – became especially associated with high quality traditional knitwears.

From the 1970s on, both Orkney and Shetland became intimately connected to the oil industry developing in the North Sea. Sullom Voe in Shetland and Flotta in Orkney were developed as oil and gas holding areas. Unlike the rest of Scotland, both sets of islands were able to deal directly with the oil companies, meaning that money and influence began to flow into the local economies. Recognising the temporary nature of the oil industry, both local councils chose to invest in the infrastructure of the islands, as well as instituting measures which would discourage and perhaps even reverse rural depopulation. At the same time, the generally unspoilt nature of the islands, along with the oil industry, encouraged in-migration by people from many different backgrounds. The relations between incomers and locals were sometimes strained. Nevertheless, the islands have probably not been as cosmopolitan since the end of the seventeenth century.

In Shetland, at least until recently, the local varieties appeared to have survived very well, often being used as the primary vehicle of speech in almost all contexts by natives. To a large extent this was due to the presence of attitudes found among speakers against *knappin*, the inappropriate use of English in contexts where Shetlandic was required (Melchers 1985). Indeed, there was considerable ongoing change in the dialect, most notably in the extension of the use of the informal *du* to include members of the parental generation and others, even if such a spread was frowned upon by some. More recently, however, particularly among the middle classes of Lerwick, the use of a Shetland-accented form of Scottish Standard English has become quite widespread even between fellow Shetlanders (Sundkvist 2004).

Orkney dialect appears to have survived less well. But since there has been very little scholarly work carried out there in recent years, most of the evidence is anecdotal. It does seem likely, however, that Shetlanders perceive their local variety as being more central to their self-perception as Shetlanders than many Orcadians do, even if there is an equivalent to Shetlandic *knappin* in Orcadian *chantin*.

5.4 Conclusion

The dialects of northern Scotland and of the Northern Isles are fairly well preserved – at least in comparison with the traditional dialects of central Scotland. This should not be taken as an invitation for self-satisfaction. The effects of the inclusion of these areas into a globalised culture and economy have been considerable and have already led to a significant loss of traditional usage – in sound, lexis and structure – which was in daily use until very recently.

There is a danger, moreover, that some aspects of dialect use – such as their employment in cultural activities – may *heritigise* the local dialect, sundering it from its former everyday use.

Whether homogenisation of language will be total, or, more likely, larger regional units of dialects will develop with some local peculiarities expressing identity within these larger groups, is beyond the subject matter of this book. It is probable, however, that these dialects will be among the last to be affected by the most sweeping of ongoing linguistic changes in Scotland.

Notes

1. Much of the preceding is based on Smith (1987) and Graham (1987). The seminal discussion on the retreat of Gaelic in Scotland is Withers (1984); Horsburgh (1997) concentrates on the same phenomenon in the North-East.
2. Much of the preceding is based upon Turnock (1987). Immigration into the area is discussed by Ditchburn and Harper (2002).

6 Survey of previous works and annotated bibliography

6.1 General histories, grammars, studies of phonology and dictionaries of Scots

There are a number of good single volume discussions of the history and use of Scots. A good idea might be to read both McClure (1997) and Jones (2002). The first is written from the perspective of an activist for the language; the latter from the perspective of a descriptive linguist who does not distinguish between 'Scots' and 'English' in contemporary Scotland. Jones (2002) does not cover some of the grammatical features which mark off Northern and Insular Scots from more southerly varieties.

Jones (1997) presents essays on aspects of the history of Scots written by experts in various fields. The level of scholarship contained in this volume is impressive to say the least. Some of the essays are a little advanced for readers with little or no background in linguistics, however. I would single out Macafee (1997) as a particularly lucid discussion of the contemporary state of, and changes in progress in, Scots, nonetheless.

The early history of Scots is especially well-covered in Macafee (2002); the lack of Celtic influence on most varieties of Scots is discussed in Macafee and Ó Baoill (1997). The history of the variety's 'decline' in the face of Standard English is handled by Aitken (1979) and Dossena (2005), among others.

The primary sources for discussion of the morphosyntax of Scots are Macafee (1992–), Beal (1997), Purves (2002) and Miller (2003). I have found Macafee's and Beal's works particularly useful in the writing of this book. The other two contributions, while excellent, have some drawbacks for the elaboration of the usage of a particular variety. Purves' work has a bias towards literary usage; Miller's work is grounded in the study of less traditional Central Scots varieties.

While most histories or descriptions of the language include a discussion of the sound patterns of the various dialects of Scots, the only systematic in-depth treatment is Johnson (1997). This thoroughness means, however, that his treatment can be rather opaque unless you have a considerable knowledge of both phonology and the dialects of Scots. In this book I have attempted to interpret Johnson's findings in a way which makes both detail and over-riding pattern more easily discernible. Abercrombie (1979) acts as a useful introduction to the social variation in accent found in Scotland when using Standard English.

Scots is blessed in having two major multi-volume dictionaries: *A Dictionary of the Older Scottish Tongue* (Craigie and Aitken 1931–2002) and *The Scottish National Dictionary* (Grant and Murison 1929–76), the former dealing largely with the period in which Scots was the main literary and governmental language of Scotland, the latter with usage in literature and speech, with particular emphasis on the nineteenth and twentieth centuries. The latter dictionary, as well as its offshoots such as *The Concise Scots Dictionary* (Robinson 1985), are excellent means of plotting meaning and usage across time and the country. As we saw in Chapter 4, however, local usage may not always match what is mapped out by the national work. This minor criticism should not be taken as in any way downplaying these works' importance, however. Equally useful are the materials assembled for *The Linguistic Atlas of Scotland* (Mather and Speitel 1985).

6.2 Local history and geography

The areas under discussion in this book are somewhat patchily served by readily available studies of local history and geography. For Shetland, I have found most useful the discussion in Schei (1988), which provides information and comment on the history, culture and environment of the islands. I have also used a range of more academic resources referred to in Chapter 5, all of which are worth investigating.

Orkney has its own History (Thomson 2001), which is both intellectually rigorous and highly readable. Beyond this, I have a particular soft spot for Mackay Brown (1969), which discusses the islands' past and present through a poet's language and imagination. An excellent – and relatively inexpensive – translation of the *Orkneyinga Saga* is available in the shape of Pálsson and Edwards (1981).

For the mainland areas discussed in this book, probably the best introductory resources are the various 'county books' edited by Omand. Intended for an informed non-scholarly audience, the essays in these collections are all written by experts in their respective fields. References for more specific places and events can be found in Chapters 2 and 5.

A resource which is often sadly overlooked is the work of local historians and geographers, often found only in booklets and photocopies available in local libraries. Every county (and often every town) has its own local collection, normally with a well-informed local studies librarian. These collections are often excellent and under-used.

6.3 Studies of specific dialects

6.3.1 Shetland

The 'death' of Shetland Norn is treated by Jakobsen (1897), Flom (1928–9), Barnes (1984 and 1998) and Rendboe (1984 and 1987). As we saw in Chapter 5, I lean towards a slightly modified version of Barnes' views. Discussions of the modern dialect can be found in Murison (1954) and Catford (1957). Jakobsen (1932) discusses the Norn element in the local variety. Graham (1993) generally succeeds in providing a broader treatment of the vocabulary of the Shetland varieties, including those words and phrases common to many Scots dialects. The best introduction to the grammar of any dialect of Scots is to be found in Robertson and Graham (1952). The prosody of both Shetland and Orkney dialects is handled in van Leyden (2004). While having many excellent points, this dissertation assumes considerable prior knowledge of phonological theory. Change in progress in the dialect is well-covered in the works of Melchers cited in this bibliography. Fishermen's *tabu* language is discussed in Fenton (1968–9 and 1987).

6.3.2 Orkney

In comparison to Shetland, the dialects of Orkney are not at all well covered. The Norn element in Orkney vocabulary is covered by Marwick (1929); Orkney Norn and its death are discussed in Barnes (1998). The modern dialect vocabulary is exemplified in the excellent Lamb (1988).

6.3.3 Caithness

The 'death' of Norn in Caithness is discussed in the highly speculative Thorsen (1954). Baldwin (1982) contains a number of interesting essays on the linguistic history and ecology of the county. Mather (1978) briefly discusses the local dialect in a paper intended for a general audience. Sutherland (1992) provides a short but informative exemplification of local dialect vocabulary. Unfortunately, this book was self-published and may not always be readily available. Wickens (1980, 1981) provides some illustrative material on knowledge of local lexis by schoolchildren. Richard (2003) discusses the maintenance of lexis in a rather more systematic way. Because this is an MA dissertation, however, it is not readily available. If you are interested in reading it, please get in touch with me.

6.3.4 The Black Isle

As ever, Black Isle dialects are something of a Cinderella in relation to the other varieties. Indeed the only source I have been able to find is the self-published King Sutherland (no date).

6.3.5 The North-East

The North-East, on the other hand, has been given considerable scholarly treatment. The central discussion of the local dialect can be found in McClure (2002). While generally excellent, there may be too strong a focus on literary usage, in particular in the Texts section of the book. The linguistic history – in particular the Gaelic heritage – of the area is treated by Horsburgh (1997). Dieth (1932) and Wölck (1965) use the methodologies of traditional dialectology to discuss the phonology of areas within the North-East. Dieth's work is particularly useful. Kynoch (2004) represents a genuine attempt to produce a dictionary of the North-East dialects. I have discussed both its positive and negative attributes in Chapter 4. I would strongly recommend Buchan and Toumin (1989). Although not intended to be scholarly, it provides the native speakers' intuition so necessary for works of this type as perceived by writers of considerable ability. It is also an enjoyable read, in comparison with many of the more populist discussions of 'the Doric' available, some of which have an unfortunate vein of mockery running through them. Fenton (1987) represents a scholarly discussion of the vocabulary of traditional agricultural life and its connection to that life. Recent language change is covered, in terms of lexis, by Downie (1983), Hendry (1997), McGarrity (1998) and Löw-Wiebach (2005), in terms of lexis and phonology by Middleton (2001). Local language attitudes are discussed by Imamura (2004).

6.4 Theoretical views discussed in this book

Underpinning a large part of this book are theoretical views on *language contact* and *language shift*, two closely related but discrete subjects. Those theoretical issues raised in this book are, I hope, also explained in the book. You may be interested in reading more, however. The following paragraphs are designed to give you some guidance in these matters.

For language contact, a good starting point is Thomason (2001), a textbook which also acts as an invitation to wider and more diverse surveys. The same author has also produced a much more demanding book, along with Kaufman (Thomason and Kaufman 1988). There can be no debate over the scholarship contained in these works; what I (along with a number of other scholars) might find fault with in these books is the regular assumption that it is whole constructions – phonological, lexical or structural – which are transferred from one language to another through contact. No doubt this is true to a large extent; in at least one of the language contact situations discussed in this book – Scots and Norse – the contact languages are also quite close relatives of each other.

A number of scholars – most notably Kerswill (for instance Kerswill and Williams 1997) – have discussed what happens in such close contact situations, finding that a great deal of *koineisation* takes place, with speakers of both varieties finding means – often through 'simplification' of one form or another – of developing mutual comprehension. Interested readers might want also to consult works by Trudgill (1983, 1986 and 2004) and Millar (2000) on these matters. Mufwene (2001) provides a fascinating discussion of how the different 'inputs' to the formation of a new variety may affect that variety's nature.

For language shift, the central theoretical prop of the book is Sasse (1992). Beyond this, Dorian (1981) is the classic study of the process of shift. Gal's 1979 study of language shift among Hungarian speakers in south-east Austria also has much of interest to say about the cultural and social domains which are most likely to encourage the retention of the 'dying' language for longest. The *doyen* of the study of language maintenance and shift is Joshua Fishman. His 1991 and 2001 books demonstrate what can actually be done to help a language retain native speakers. From a negative point of view his ideas on how to save a language can also be employed to see how a language loses speakers; in particular, the loss (or lack) of literacy and the end of transfer of the language from one generation to another.

6.5 Suggestions for future research

Although a considerable amount of often very impressive scholarship has been focused on the dialects discussed in this book, anyone who considers the present sum of knowledge will find what needs to be done daunting.

Some of the dialects have had practically no scholarly work carried out at all. This is especially the case with the dialects of the Black Isle where, apart from some phonological work (which included some lexical collection as well), carried out as part of a Scotland-wide survey, little is known. This is particularly pressing for this area, because surviving speakers of at least the densest forms of the local dialect are now elderly.

Caithness is also relatively poor in scholarly treatments, although, in general, there is greater evidence for scholarly interest in the dialect. The unique phonology of Caithness deserves more research; again, it is under threat from more mainstream varieties, with the best speakers now being elderly.

Although Orkney has an excellent dictionary of its dialect, it has provoked nothing like the scholarly interest which Shetland has. Certainly work on the very local phonological and lexical variation found in the islands would be very welcome, essentially as an update of the findings of the *Linguistic Atlas*, factoring in the after-effects of large-scale economic change and population movement in a globalised world.

Shetland has been well-served by scholarship. I hope that this trend continues. Much needs to be done, however; not least studies of highly localised vowel quality and quantity issues. Although some work on the breakdown of the old dialect-speaking system has been carried out, many questions remain unanswered. There is also need for a discussion of the Shetlandic movement and its attempts at a form of written standardisation.

Much has already been achieved for the North-East as well. It is a great pity, however, that the second volume of Dieth's *Grammar* was not completed. Beyond this, much still needs to be done: on the effects of large-scale immigration; on the survival of occupation-specific lexis in the aftermath of change. A study of the Doric movement and its ideology would also be welcome.

With all of these dialects, there is tremendous need for work on lexical change. Of all of the chapters of this book that on lexis was the most difficult to write and is undoubtedly the least satisfactory. A case could be made for a large-scale project involving a number of scholars dealing with the different areas. Such a project would need extensive funding; the length of time needed to complete it might be unacceptable in the present research climate.

To a lesser extent, elements of the grammars of all these varieties deserve greater attention. The use of *this* and *that* as plural demonstratives throughout the region, and their competition with standard and colloquial English equivalents, would make for a particularly important study. Work on these dialects should not, and will not, be confined to professional scholars. It is open to anyone who lives in these regions to start surveys of their own. There is much to do, not much time and too few scholars.

6.6 Works cited in this chapter and the book as a whole

Abercrombie, David (1979), 'The accents of Standard English in Scotland', in Aitken and McArthur (1979), pp. 68–84.

Aitken, A. J. (1979), 'Scottish speech: a historical view, with special reference to the Standard English of Scotland', in Aitken and McArthur (eds), pp. 85–118.

Aitken, A. J. (1981), 'The Scottish vowel-length rule', in Benskin and Samuels, pp. 131–57.

Aitken, A. J. and Tom McArthur (eds) (1979), *Languages of Scotland*, Edinburgh: Chambers.

Amini, Marjan (1998), 'Use of Same polarity tags in Aberdeen and the North East of Scotland', unpublished MLitt dissertation, University of Aberdeen.

Anthony, Richard (1997), *Herds and Hinds: Farm Labour in Lowland Scotland, 1900–1939*, Phantassie, East Linton: Tuckwell.

Ash, Marinell (1991), *This Noble Harbour: A History of the Cromarty Firth*, ed. James Macaulay and Margaret A. Mackay, Edinburgh: John Donald.

Baldwin, John R. (ed.) (1982), *Caithness: A Cultural Crossroads*, Edinburgh: Edina Press.

Barnes, Michael P. (1984), 'Orkney and Shetland Norn', in Trudgill (ed.), pp. 352–66.

Barnes, Michael P. (1998), *The Norn Language of Shetland and Orkney*, Lerwick: Shetland Times.

Beal, Joan (1997), 'Syntax and morphology', in Jones (ed.), pp. 335–77.

Benskin, Michael and M. L. Samuels (eds) (1981), *So Meny People Longages and Tonges*, Edinburgh: privately published.

Black, Diane (2003), 'The demonstrative pronouns in Caithness: a sociolinguistic study', unpublished MA dissertation, University of Aberdeen.

Boelmans Kranenburg, H. A. H. (1983), 'The Netherlands fisheries and the Shetland Islands', in Withrington (ed.), pp. 96–106.

Brenzinger, Matthias (ed.) (1992), *Language Death: Factual and Theoretical Explorations with Special Reference to East Africa*, Berlin and New York: Mouton de Gruyter.

Buchan, Peter and David Toulmin (1989), *Buchan Claik: The Saut an the Glaur o't: A Compendium of Words and Phrases from the North-East of Scotland*, Edinburgh: Gordon Wright.

Campbell, Roy H. (1985), *Scotland since 1707: The Rise of an Industrial Society* (2nd edn), Edinburgh: Donald.

Catford, J. C. (1957), 'Shetland dialect', *Shetland Folk Book* 3: 71–5.

Corbett, John, J. Derrick McClure and Jane Stuart-Smith (eds) (2003), *The Edinburgh Companion to Scots*, Edinburgh: Edinburgh University Press.

Craigie, William A. and A. J. Aitken (eds) (1931–2002), *A Dictionary of the Older Scottish Tongue* (12 vols), Chicago: University of Chicago Press/Aberdeen: Aberdeen University Press/Oxford: Oxford University Press.

CSD: see Robinson (1985).

Cummins, W. A. (1995), *The Age of the Picts*, Stroud: Alan Sutton.

Dennison, E. Patricia, David Ditchburn and Michael Lynch (eds) (2002), *Aberdeen before 1800*, East Linton: Tuckwell.

Devine, Tom M. (1995), *Exploring the Scottish Past: Themes in the History of Scottish Society*, East Linton: Tuckwell.

Dieth, Eugen (1932), *A Grammar of the Buchan Dialect (Aberdeenshire), Descriptive and Historical*, Cambridge: W. Heffer.

Ditchburn, David and Marjory Harper (2002), 'Aberdeen and the outside world', in Dennison, Ditchburn and Lynch, pp. 377–407.

Donaldson, Gordon (1983), 'The Scots settlement in Shetland', in Withrington, pp. 8–19.

Dorian, Nancy C. (1981), *Language Death: The Life Cycle of a Scottish Gaelic Dialect*, Philadelphia: University of Pennsylvania Press.

Dossena, Marina (2005), *Scotticisms in Grammar and Vocabulary*, Edinburgh: Donald.

Downie, Anne (1983), 'The survival of the fishing dialects on the Moray Firth', *Scottish Language* 2: 42–8.

Dunbavin, Paul (1998), *Picts and Ancient Britons: An Exploration of Pictish Origins*, Nottingham: Third Millenium.

Ejerhed, E. and I. Henrysson (eds) (1980), *Tvåspråkighet*, Umeå: Umeå University.

Fasold, Ralph (1984), *The Sociolinguistics of Society*, Oxford: Blackwell.

Fenton, Alexander (1968–9), 'The Tabu language of the fishermen of Orkney and Shetland', *Ethnologia Europaea* 2–3: 118–22.

Fenton, Alexander (1978), *The Northern Isles: Orkney and Shetland*, Edinburgh: Donald.

Fenton, Alexander (1987), *Wirds an' Wark 'e Seasons roon on an Aberdeenshire Farm*, Aberdeen: Aberdeen University Press.

Ferguson, Charles A. (1959), 'Diglossia', *Word* 15: 325–40.

Filippula, Markku (1999), *Grammar of Irish English: Language in Hibernian Style*, London: Routledge.

Fishman, Joshua A. (1991), *Reversing Language Shift*, Clevedon: Multilingual Matters.

Fishman, Joshua A. (ed.) (2001), *Can Threatened Languages Be Saved? Reversing Language Shift Revisited: A 21st Century Perspective*, Clevedon: Multilingual Matters.

Fitzgerald, Colleen M. (2002), 'Vowel harmony in Buchan Scots English', *English Language and Linguistics* 6: 61–79.

Flom, George T. (1928–9), 'The transition from Norse to Lowland Scotch in Shetland, 1600–1850. A study in the decay of one language and its influence upon the language that supplanted it', *Saga Book of the Viking Society* 10: 145–64.

Forsyth, Katherine (1997), *Language in Pictland*, Utrecht: de keltische Draak.

Fraser, James E. (2002), *The Battle of Dunnichen 685*, Stroud: Tempus.

Friedland, Klaus (1983), 'Hanseatic merchants and their trade with Shetland', in Withrington, pp. 86–95.

Gal, Susan (1979), *Language Shift: Social Determinants of Linguistic Change in Bilingual Austria*, New York: Academic Press.

Görlach, Manfred (1987), 'Colonial Lag? The alleged conservative character of American English and other "colonial" varieties', *English World-Wide* 8: 41–60.

Görlach, Manfred (ed.) (1985), *Focus on: Scotland*, 'Varieties of English Around the World' 5, Amsterdam: Benjamins.

Graham, Cuthbert (1987), 'Castle Country', in Omand, pp. 151–64.

Graham, John J. (1993), *The Shetland Dictionary* (3rd edn), Lerwick: Shetland Times.

Grant, William and David D. Murison (eds) (1929–76), *The Scottish National Dictionary*, Edinburgh: Scottish National Dictionary Association (= *SND*).

Hægstad, M (ed.) (1900), *Hildinakvadet*, 'Videnskabsselskabets Skrifter II: Historisk-filosofiske Klasse 2', Christiania [Oslo]: Dybwad.

Hamilton, Henry (ed.) (1960), *The County of Aberdeen*, the third *Statistical Account of Scotland* 7, Glasgow: Collins.

Hendry, Ian D. (1997), 'Doric – an investigation into its use amongst primary school children in the North East of Scotland', unpublished MLitt dissertation, University of Aberdeen.

Horsburgh, David (1997), 'Gaelic language and culture in north-east Scotland: a diachronic study', unpublished PhD dissertation, University of Aberdeen.

Imamura, Mari (2004), 'Primary school teachers' attitudes towards the Scots language in education', unpublished PhD dissertation, University of Aberdeen.

Jackson, Kenneth (1955), 'The Pictish language', in Wainwright, pp. 129–66.

Jackson, Kenneth (1972), *The Gaelic Notes in the 'Book of Deer'*, Cambridge: Cambridge University Press.

Jakobsen, Jakob (1897), *The Dialect and Place Names of Shetland: Two Popular Lectures*, Lerwick: Manson.

Jakobsen, Jakob (1932), *An Etymological Dictionary of the Norn Language in Shetland* (2 vols), London: David Nutt/Copenhagen: Vilhelm Prior.

Jedrej, M. Charles and Mark Nuttall (1996), *White Settlers: The Impact Of Rural Repopulation in Scotland*, Newark, NJ: Harwood Academic Publishers.

Johnson, Paul (1997), 'Regional variation', in Jones, pp. 433–513.

Jones, Charles (2002), *The English Language in Scotland: An Introduction to Scots*, East Linton: Tuckwell.

Jones, Charles (ed.) (1997), *The Edinburgh History of the Scots Language*, Edinburgh: Edinburgh University Press.

Joseph, John Earl (1987), *Eloquence and Power: The Rise Of Language Standards and Standard Languages*, London: Pinter.

Kerswill, P. and A. Williams (1997), 'Creating a new town koine: children and language change in Milton Keynes', *Reading Working Papers in Linguistics* 3: 205–57.

King Sutherland, David (n.d.), *Fisherlore of Avoch*, privately published.

Knooihuizen, Remco (2006), 'The Norn to Scots language shift: another look at the evidence', *Northern Studies* 39: 5–16.

Kynoch, Douglas (2004), *A Doric Dictionary* (2nd edn), Dalkieth: Scottish Cultural Press.

Laing, Margaret (ed.) (1989), *Middle English Dialectology: Essays on Some Principles and Problems*. Aberdeen: Aberdeen University Press.

Lamb, Gregor (1988), *Orkney Wordbook: A Dictionary of the Dialect of Orkney*, Birsay, Orkney: Byrgisey.

Lorvik, Marjorie (2003), 'Mutual intelligibility of timber trade terminology in the North Sea countries during the time of the "Scottish Trade"', *Nordic Journal of English Studies* 2: 223–44.

Löw-Wiebach, Danielle A. V. (2005), *Language Attitudes and Language Use in Pitmedden (Aberdeenshire)*, Bern: Lang.

Macafee, Caroline I. (1989), 'Middle Scots dialects – extrapolating backwards', in McClure and Spiller, pp. 429–41.

Macafee, Caroline I. (1992–), 'Characteristics of Non-Standard Grammar in Scotland', http://www.abdn.ac.uk/-enl038/grammar.htm

Macafee, Caroline I. (1994), *Traditional dialect in the modern world: a Glasgow case study*, Frankfurt am Main: Lang.

Macafee, Caroline I. (1997), 'Ongoing change in modern Scots', in Jones, pp. 514–48.

Macafee, Caroline I. (2002), 'A history of Scots to 1700', in Craigie and Aikton, vol. 12, 1931–2002, pp. xxi–clvi.

Macafee, C. I. and Colm Ó Baoill (1997), 'Why Scots is not a Celtic English', in Tristram, pp. 245–87.

Macaulay, Ronald K. S. (2005), *Extremely Common Eloquence: Constructing Scottish Identity through Narrative*, 'Scottish Cultural Review of Language and Literature' 3, Amsterdam: Rodopi.

McClure, J. D. (1977), 'Vowel duration in a Scottish accent', *Journal of the International Phonetic Association* 7: 10–16.

McClure, J. D. (1987), 'Dialect speech', in Omand, pp. 306–15.

McClure, J. D. (1997), *Why Scots Matters* (2nd edn), Edinburgh: Saltire Society.

McClure, J. D. (2002), *Doric: The Dialect of North-East Scotland*, Amsterdam: Benjamins.

McClure, J. D. (ed.) (2004), *Doonsin' Emerauds: New Scrieves anent Scots and Gaelic/ New Studies in Scots and Gaelic*, Belfast: Cló Ollscoil na Banríona.

McClure, J. D. and Michael R. G. Spiller (eds) (1989), *Bryght Lanternis: Essays on the Language and Literature of Medieval and Renaissance Scotland*, Aberdeen: Aberdeen University Press.

McGarrity, Briege (1998), 'A sociolinguistic study of attitudes towards and proficiency in the Doric dialect in Aberdeen', unpublished MPhil dissertation, University of Aberdeen.

Mackay Brown, George (1969), *An Orkney Tapestry*, London: Gollancz.

McRae, Sandra Mhairi (2000), 'The demonstrative pronouns in the North-East: an introductory discussion', *Scottish Language* 19: 66–82.

McRae, Sandra Mhairi (2004), 'Demonstrative use and variation in the Lower Garioch', in McClure, pp. 60–7.

Marren, Peter (1990), *Grampian Battles: The Historic Battles of North East Scotland from AD84 to 1745*, Edinburgh: Mercat Press.

Marshall, Jonathan (2003), 'The changing sociolinguistic status of the glottal stop in northeast Scottish English', *English World-Wide* 24: 89–108.

Marwick, Hugh (1929), *The Orkney Norn*, Oxford: Oxford University Press.

Mather, J. Y. (1978), 'The dialect of Caithness', *Scottish Literary Journal Supplement* 6: 1–16.

Mather, J. Y. and H. H. Speitel (eds) (1975–85), *The Linguistic Atlas of Scotland* (3 vols), London: Croom Helm.

Melchers, Gunnel (1980), 'The Norn element in Shetland dialect today – a case of "never accepted" language death', in Ejerhed and Henrysson, pp. 254–61.

Melchers, Gunnel (1985), '"Knappin'", "Proper English", "Modified Scottish", Some language attitudes in the Shetland Isles', in Görlach, pp. 86–105.

Melchers, Gunnel (1986), 'Narrowing and extension of meaning in the Scandinavian-based vocabulary of Shetland dialect', *Scottish Language* 5: 110–19.

Melchers, Gunnel (1991), 'Norn-Scots: a complicated language contact situation in Shetland', in Ureland and Broderick, pp. 110–19.

Middleton, Sheena Booth (2001), 'A Study into the knowledge and use of Scots amongst primary pupils on Upper Deeside', unpublished MLitt dissertation, University of Aberdeen.

Millar, Robert McColl (1996), 'Gaelic-influenced Scots in pre-Revolutionary Maryland', in Ureland and Clarkson, pp. 387–410.

Millar, Robert McColl (1999), 'Some geographical and cultural patterns in the lexical/semantic structure of Scots', *Northern Scotland* 18: 55–65.

Millar, Robert McColl (2000), *System Collapse System Rebirth: The Demonstrative Pronouns of English and the Rise of the Definite Article 950–1350*, Bern: Lang.

Millar, Robert McColl (2004), 'Linguistic history on the margins of the Germanic-speaking world: some preliminary thoughts', in McClure, pp. 3–17.

Millar, Robert McColl (2005), *Language, Nation and Power*, Basingstoke: Palgrave Macmillan.

Miller, Jim (2003), 'Syntax and discourse in modern scots', in Corbett, McClure and Stuart-Smith, pp. 72–109.

Milne, J. (1947), *Twixt Ury and Don and Round About*, Inverurie Aberdeenshire: Dufton Scott and Son.

Mowat, Ian R. M. (1981), *Easter Ross 1750–1850: The Double Frontier*, Edinburgh: Donald.

Mufwene, Saliko S. (2001), *The Ecology of Language Evolution*, Cambridge: Cambridge University Press.

Murison, David (1954), 'Scots speech in Shetland', in Simpson, pp. 255–60.

Murison, David (1963), 'Local dialects', in O'Dell and Mackintosh, pp. 197–202.

Nicolaisen, W. F. H. (1976), *Scottish Place-names: Their Study and Significance*, London: Batsford.

Nicolaisen, W. F. H. (1982), 'Scandinavians and Celts in Caithness: the place-name evidence', in Baldwin, pp. 75–85.

O'Dell, A. C. and J. Mackintosh (eds) (1963), *The North-East of Scotland*, Aberdeen: Central Press.

Omand, Donald (1987), *The Grampian Book*, Golspie, Sutherland: Northern Times.

Omand, Donald (1989), *The New Caithness Book*, Wick, Caithness: North of Scotland Newspapers.

Omand, Donald (ed.) (1984), *The Ross and Cromarty Book*, Golspie, Sutherland: Northern Times.

Omond, James (1911; 1980), *Orkney Eighty Years Ago (with Special Reference to Evie)*, Kirkwall: Kirkwall Press.

Pálsson, Hermann and Paul Edwards (eds) (1981), '*Orkneyinga saga*: *The History of the Earls of Orkney*, Harmondsworth: Penguin.

Paster, Mary (2004), 'Vowel height harmony in Buchan Scots', *Phonology* 21: 359–407.

Pavlenko, Alexander (1997), 'The origin of the *be* perfect with transitives in the Shetland dialect', *Scottish Language* 16: 88–96.

Pollner, C. (1985), *Englisch in Livingston: Ausgewählte sprachliche Erscheinungen in einer schottischen New Town*, Frankfurt am Main: Lang.

Price, Glanville (2000a), 'Pictish', in Price (2000b), pp. 127–31.

Price, Glanville (ed.) (2000b), *Languages in Britain and Ireland*, Oxford: Blackwell.

Purves, David (2002), *A Scots Grammar: Scots Grammar and Usage* (2nd edn), Edinburgh: Saltire Society.

Ralston, Ian (1987), 'Iron Age to Middle Ages', in Omand, pp. 131–9.

Rendboe, Laurits (1984), 'How "worn out" or "corrupted" was Shetland Norn in its final stage', *NOWELE* 3: 53–88.

Rendboe, Laurits (1987), *Det gamle shetlandske sprog. George Low's ordliste fra 1774*, NOWELE Supplement Volume 3, Odense: Odense universitetsforlag.

Richard, Jan Lauren (2003), 'Investigating lexical change in Caithness', unpublished MA dissertation, University of Aberdeen.

Robinson, Mairi (ed.) (1985), *The Concise Scots Dictionary*, Aberdeen: Aberdeen University Press (= *CSD*).

Robertson, T. A. and John J. Graham (1952), *Grammar & Usage of the Shetland Dialect*, Lerwick: Shetland Times.

Samuels, M. L. (1989), 'The Great Scandinavian Belt', in Laing, pp. 106–15.

Sasse, Hans-Jürgen (1992), 'Theory of language death', in Brenzinger, pp. 7–30.

Schei, Liv Kjørsvik (1988), *The Shetland Story*, London: Batsford.

Shepherd, Ian (1987), 'The early peoples', in Omand, pp. 119–30.

Simpson, Grant G. (ed.) (1990), *Scotland and Scandinavia 800–1800*, Edinburgh: John Donald.

Simpson, W. Douglas (ed.) (1954), *The Viking Congress, Lerwick 1950*, Edinburgh: Oliver and Boyd.

Smith, Brian (1990), 'Shetland, Scandinavia, Scotland 1300–1700: the changing nature of contact', in Simpson, pp. 25–37.

Smith, Brian (1996), 'The development of the spoken and written Shetland dialect: a historian's view', in Waugh, pp. 30–43.

Smith, Hance D. (1984), *Shetland Life and Trade*, Edinburgh: John Donald.

Smith, John S. (1987), 'The Middle Ages', in Omand, pp. 151–64.

Smith, Jennifer (2000), '"You ø na hear o' that kind o' things": negative *do* in Buckie Scots', *English World-Wide* 21: 231–59.

Smyth, Alfred P. (1984), *Warlords and Holy Men: Scotland AD 80–100*. Edinburgh: Edinburgh University Press.

SND: see Grant and Murison (1929–76)

Sundkvist, Peter B. (2004), *The Vowel System of a Shetland Accent of Scottish Standard English: A Segmental Analysis*, Stockholm: Stockholm University Department of English.

Sutherland, Iain (1992), *The Caithness Dictionary*, Wick, Caithness: privately published.

Telford, Susan (1998), *In a Warld a wir Ane: A Shetland Herring Girl's Story*, Lerwick: Shetland Times.

Thomason, Sarah Grey (2001), *Language Contact: An Introduction*, Edinburgh: Edinburgh University Press.

Thomason, Sarah Grey and Terrence Kaufman (1988), *Language Contact, Creolization and Genetic Linguistics*, Berkeley: University of California Press.

Thomson, William P. L. (2001), *The New History of Orkney*, Edinburgh: Mercat Press.

Thorsen, Per (1954), 'The third Norn dialect – that of Caithness', in Simpson, pp. 230–8.

Tristram, Hildegard L. C. (ed.) (1997), *The Celtic Englishes*, Heidelberg: Winter.

Trudgill, Peter (1983), *On Dialect*, Oxford: Blackwell.

Trudgill, Peter (1986), *Dialects in Contact*, Oxford: Blackwell.

Trudgill, Peter (2004), *New-dialect Formation: The Inevitability of Colonial Englishes*, Edinburgh: Edinburgh University Press.

Trudgill, Peter (ed.) (1984), *Language in the British Isles*, Cambridge: Cambridge University Press.

Turnock, David (1987), 'Early Modern Times', in Omand, pp. 165–80.

Ureland, P. Sture and George Braderick (eds) (1991) *Language Contact in the British Isles*, Tübingen: Narr.

Ureland, P. Sture and Iain Clarkson (eds) (1996), *Language Contact across the North Atlantic*, Tübingen: Niemeyer

van Leyden, Klaske (2004), *Prosodic Characteristics of Orkney and Shetland Dialects: An Experimental Approach*, Utrecht: Lot.

Wainwright, F. T. (ed.) (1955), *The Problem of the Picts*, Edinburgh: Thomas Nelson.

Waugh, Doreen J. (ed.) (1996) *Shetland's Northern Links: Language and History*, Edinburgh: Scottish Society for Northern Studies.

Wells, J. C. (1982), *Accents of English* (3 vols), Cambridge: Cambridge University Press.

Wickens, Beatrice (1980), 'Caithness speech: studying the dialect with the help of school children', *Scottish Literary Journal Supplement* 12: 61–76.

Wickens, Beatrice (1981), 'Caithness speech: studying the dialect with the help of school children (Part II)', *Scottish Literary Journal Supplement* 14: 25–36.

Withers, Charles W. J. (1984), *Gaelic 1698–1981: The Geographical History of a Language*, Edinburgh: John Donald.

Withrington, Donald J. (ed.) (1983), *Shetland and the Outside World 1469–1969*. Oxford: Oxford University Press.

Wölck, Wolfgang (1965), *Phonematische Analyse der Sprache von Buchan*, Heidelberg: Winter.

7 Texts

In the following texts I have attempted to provide as comprehensive as possible a 'snapshot' of local speech norms throughout northern Scotland and the Northern Isles in the last year or so. Inevitably this has meant that more examples could be given of present-day Shetland dialect than of the dialects of the Black Isle, since the dialect is very much alive in the cultural and social lives of people on the various islands and regions of the archipelago. For each sample, I have provided a transcription into a Scots form of English spelling, a broad phonemic transcription and a discussion of the particularly noteworthy features of the informant's speech. Where words or phrases are used which are not normal outside the Scots-speaking world (or are confined to a particular Scots dialect), a glossary is provided after the first transcription.

7.1 Shetland

7.1.1 George Jamieson, Unst, October 2005

George Jamieson: When A wis born here an brought up here on i croft – ma father wis a crofter all his life, came here in twenty-eight . . .
Millar: Ay.
George Jamieson: . . . set up the . . . built the house an de wee steeding doon there. And so you were born in a situation, an did things in a situation, where the usage o de dialect wis much stronger obviously than now . . . o . . . We were using ponies or mares – there wis no such word as *ponies* on Unst whin A wis young – which we used as work ponies. So we were harrowin an usin swingle-trees an all the bits an pieces o the crofts, an things, an dennin spades and kwat-no, takin our peats home from the hill on ponies.

steeding – homestead, smallholding; *swingle-trees*: the crossbars on a plough to which the reins controlling draught animals were connected; *dennin spades*: spades used in the harvesting of peats for fuel; *kwat-no*: 'what not'.

149

George Jamieson:
/ʍɪn a wɪz bɔrn hir
ən brɔt ʌp hir ɔn ə krɔft
ma 'faðər wɪz ə 'krɔftər ɔl ɪz ləif
kem hir ɪn 'twɪnti et/
Millar:
/ae/
George Jamieson:
/sɛt ʌp ðə
bɪlt ðə həus ən də wi 'stidɪŋ dun ðer
an so ju wər bɔrn ɪn ə sɪtju'eʃən ən dɪd θɪŋz ɪn ə sɪtju'eʃən
ʍer ðə 'juzɪdʒ ə də 'daeəlɛkt wəz mʌtʃ 'strɔŋgər ɔbvi'ʌsli ðan nəu
ɔ
wi wər 'juziŋ 'poniz
ər mers
ðer wəz no sʌtʃ wʌrd əz 'poniz ɔn ʌnst ʍin a wɪz jʌŋ
ʍitʃ wi juzd əz wʌrk 'poniz
so wi wər 'haroɪn ən 'juzin 'swɪŋgəl triz ən ɔl ðə bɪts ən 'pisis i ðə
   krɔfts
ən θɪŋz
ən 'dɛnɪn spedz ən kwat no
'tekɪn əur pits hom frɔm ðə hɪl ɔn 'poniz /

In general, George Jamieson's speech – at least as represented in this sample – is the closest of the Shetland informants to SSE. This may be due to the observer's paradox being particularly strong where the informant is a former headteacher. Nevertheless, his speech does have many specifically Shetland – if not actually Unst – features. Although he mainly employs /ð/, there are occasions when he employs Shetland /d/. Interestingly, this often occurs when he becomes animated about past events. His speech demonstrates merger or near-merger between MATE-HAME and DRESS and also GOAT, CAUGHT and COT. He also has one example – /'stidɪŋ/ – where BEAT is pronounced at /i/ rather than the Standard /ɛ/. He also has one example of /kw/ for SSE /ʍ/, a feature which certainly marks him off as being from the northern parts of Shetland. Again, it may be significant that he is talking about his past when this usage is realised.

7.1.2 Mary-Ellen Odie, Yell, October 2005

Mary-Ellen Odie: I dö a lot o genealogy, cause it's a göd subject. It gets you lökin at geography even, if you want ti see where in Lindesteen somebody came from.

Millar: Ay.

Mary-Ellen Odie: You'd go there, and it's great. It's a göd habby.

Well, anyway. So when I tök up this study, then . . . uh . . . I couldn't find anything but patronymic names. An even ma great . . . ma grannie's grannie, to make it simpler, she married yösin Robertson and she died as a Hoseson. But the people all called her Cheedie Chonster.

Millar: Ay.

Mary-Ellen Odie: An that nailed her, cause she wis John Robertson's daughter. So you can see what a recent difficulty they'd been having. That wis . . . eh . . . That particular family had had a real difficulty cause they were as stiff as the devil, and they wouldn't give in ti each other, so that the daughter at married John Robertson wis wan o the hard cases o the parish. So that's the . . . that's the way o things there. Anyway, through her A wis lökin all this patronymics. An thank God that my great granny an my father's side came from Fetlar. An shö browt wi her jöst a whole load of lovely words. We yöst ti think: 'Granny maks them up!'

yöst ti: used to

Mary-Ellen Odie: /ae dy ə lat o tʃiniˈalɔtʃi kəz ats ə gyd sʌbˈtʃɛkt
ɪt gɛts ju ˈlykən at ˈtʃiɔgrəfi ˈivən ɪf ju want tə si ʍer ɪn ˈlɪnəstin ˈsʌmbɔdi kem frɔm/

Millar:
/ae/

Mary-Ellen Odie:
/jud go ðer
an ɪts gret
ɪts ə gyd ˈhabi
wɛl ˈɛni wae
so ʍɛn ae tyk ʌp ə ðɪs ˈstʌdi
ðɛn ə ae ˈkydənt faend ˈɛni θɪŋ bʌt patˈronɪmɪk nemz
ən ˈivən ma gret
ma ˈgraniz ˈgrani tə mek ɪt ˈsɪmplər
ʃi ˈmarid dʒɔn ˈrɔbərtsən
and ʃi daed əz ə ˈhozesən
bʌt ðə ˈpipəl ɔl kɔld hɪr ˈtʃidi ˈtʃɔnstər/
Millar:
/ae/
Mary-Ellen Odie:
/ən ðat neld hɪr
kɔz ʃi wɪs tʃɔn ˈrɔbərtsɪnz ˈdɔtər

so ju kən si ʍat ə 'risənt 'dɪfikʌlti ðed bin 'havɪŋ
ðat wɪz ə
ðat par'tikjulər 'faməli had had ə ril 'dɪfikʌlti kʌz ðe wɛr əz stɪf əz ðə
    'dɪvəl
ən ðe wudənt gɪv ɪn tə itʃ 'ʌðər
so ðat ðə 'dɔtər ət 'marid 'jyzən 'rɔbərtsɪn wɪz wan o ðə hard 'kɛsiz o
    ðə 'parɪʃ
so ðats ðə
ðats ðə we ə θɪŋz ðer
'ɛni we θru hɪr a wɪz lukən ɔl ðɪs pat'ronɪmɪks
an θaŋk gɔd ðat mae grɛt 'grani an mae 'faðərz saed kem frɔm 'fɛtlar
ən ʃy brəut we hɪr dʒyst ə hol lod əv 'lʌvli wʌrdz
ae
wi jyst ti θɪŋk
'grani maks ðɪm ʌp/

In many ways, Mary Ellen Odie was the Shetlander who accommodated most. This is most striking in her two pronunciations of *make*. The more local pronunciation /maks/ is confined to reported speech from her childhood. She also always uses SSE /ð/ initially. It may be significant that, in another part of her interview, she says that she is quite sanguine about language change in Shetland, a phenomenon which most other informants regretted.

Nevertheless, her speech is full of local features, including diphthongisation of the <ough> words (/brəut/), merger or near merger between MATE-HAME and DRESS and between GOAT and CAUGHT, devoicing of /dʒ/ to /tʃ/ and the use of plural *this*.

7.1.3 *Marina Irvine and Nettie Arthur, Whalsay, October 2005*

Marina Irvine: . . . pöt in mind o wir teachers, at dey wir some o de teachers at ye really got into trouble fir no spikkin English.
Millar: Mhmhm.
Marina Irvine: Ye got into trouble if you jöst spoke in . . . in your aan Shetland.
Isobel Johnson: That would be cruel to do that.
Marina Irvine: Dat wis de . . . A mind dat did happen. Bit A suppose in a sense they wir tryin ti larn you the right wey ti spik so that that mebbe wis a help later on, I . . .
Nettie Arthur: I wis at a reunion of . . . of forty-year-olds who aksed me to come to their reunion – they had a meal in the restaurant. And we were reminiscin aboot things and I said to one, 'I mind the day that I was döin

the dinner duty an du wis no gyaan tö et dee . . . dee beans at wis there wi the sausage meat and beans. An A could see dat du wis no gaan ti et it. And I came across, an du sörley tocht dat du wöd gie me de göd news first, an du said: 'Please, miss: I like peas [laughter], but I can no et the . . . the bones [laughter]. Our Whalsay weys . . . Shetland . . . *beens* mean *bones.*

mind: remember; *gyaan/gaan tö et*: going to eat; *sörley*: surely; *tocht*: thought

Marina Irvine:
/pyt mi ɪn maend o wɪr 'titʃərs
at de wɪr sʌm o də 'titʃərs
ju 'rili gɔt 'ɪntə 'trʌbl fʌr no 'spɪkən 'ɪŋglɪʃ
ju gɔt 'ɪntə 'trʌbl ɪf ju tʃyst spok ɪn ɪn jur an 'ʃetlənd/
Isobel Johnson: /ðat wud bi krul tə du ðat/
Marina Irvine:
/dat wɪz də
a maend dat dɪd 'hapən
bɪt a sə'pos ɪn ə sɛns ðe wɪr 'traeən tə larn jə ðə raet wae tə
    spɪk
so ðat 'mɪbi wɪz ə hɛlp 'letər ɔn
ae/
Nettie Arthur:
/a wɪz at ə ri'junjən əv əv 'fɔrti jir oldz
hu akst mi tə kʌm tə ðer ri'junjən
ðe had ə mil ɪn ðə 'rɛstərɔnt
ən wi wɛr 'rɛmənɪsən ə'but θɪŋs
ən ae sɛd tə wʌn
a maend ðə de ðat ae wɪz 'dyən ðə 'dɪnər 'djuti
ən du wɪz no gjan tə et di di binz
ət wɪz ðer wi ðə 'sasədʒ mit ən binz
ən a kud si dat du wɪz no gon tə et ɪt
ən ae kem ə'krɔs
ən du 'ʃyrli tɔxt du wyd gi mi də gyd njuz fɪrst
ən du sɛd
pliz mɪs
ae laek piz
bɪt a kan no et ðə ðə bonz
əur 'ʍɔlse waez
'ʃetlənd
binz minz bonz/

In the first place it should be noted that both main speakers use both

Standard English and Shetland features in their speech. It can be assumed that this was partly due to the presence of *Soothmoothers*, towards whom they were accommodating, but it seems likely that both patterns are integral parts of their idiolects. Of the two, Nettie Arthur code-switches most. A large part of her speech is quite close to the SSE end of the Shetland continuum; her recounting of the conversation at the reunion includes quite dense passages and others which, while still dialectal, are less local. Good examples of this are the two equivalents of *going*. /gjan/ and /gon/. Code-switching is also a feature of Marina Irvine's speech, however. Although she regularly realises /d/ in contexts where SSE would have /ð/, the Standard phoneme does occasionally get used. The difference between the two women's speech can perhaps be explained by the fact that Nettie Arthur had the linguistic authority (and probably ability) of a schoolteacher.

A number of very typical Shetland features pepper the text. In terms of phonology, the lack of a BITE:TRY distinction is very noticeable, as is the regular 'low' pronunciation of MEAT (occasionally diph-thongised with BAIT) and GOAT, the presence of high front rounded BUIT vowels and, as already noted, the use of /d/ where the Standard has /ð/. The same is probably true of COT, CAUGHT and GOAT. The confusion of initial voiced and voiceless affricates can be heard in *jöst*, which may begin with /tʃ/. Marina Irvine uses the typically Shetland *dey wir* where the Standard would have *there were*. Both consistently make a distinction between informal singular *du* and formal or plural *ye/you*. *Aks* for *ask* is, in terms of Scots, a marked Shetland feature.

The most notably Whalsay feature in their speech is the palatalisation of *gyaan* /gjan/.

7.1.4 Mary Blance, Lerwick (originally from the northern mainland of Shetland), October 2005

Mary Blance: I have a country, a rural, tongue, an Leruck his got its own very distinctive accents. An you'll fin a whole lot o different accents, different weys o speech within Lerwick itsel . . . em. An some o de dis-tinctiveness . . . wan o the Lerwick tongues is whit wi wid caa the Scottie Lerwick.

Millar: An whit does that mean?

Mary Blance: It's de wey dey spik, de folk dat cam in fae the nor-east o Scotland in de erli twentieth century – cam up fae . . . hmm . . . Cumrie [possibly Gamrie, an area of coastal Banffshire] an aa that kind o places . . . um . . . just following the herring.

Millar: Ay, ay. An their tongues kinna carried on a wee bit?

Mary Blance: Yas, yas. Du mean the names o the Watts, the Wisemans; there's lots o different names that ye'll come across kwaar de folk originally cam up, an that.

Mary Blance:

/ae hav ə 'kʌntri ə 'rurəl tʌŋ ən 'lɛruk hʌs got ɪts on 'vɛri dɪ'stɪŋktəv 'aksənts

ən jul fɪn ə hol lɔt o 'dɪfrənt 'aksənts 'dɪfrənt waez o spitʃ wɪθ'ɪn 'lɛrwɪk it'sɛl

əm

an sʌm o də dəs'tɪŋktɪvnəs

wan o ðə 'lɛrwɪk tʌŋz ɪz ʌit wi wɪd ka ðə 'skɔti 'lɛrwɪk/

Millar:

/ən ʌʌt dʌz ðat min/

Mary Blance:

/ɪts də wae de spɪk də fok dat kam ɪn fe ðə nɔr ist o 'skɔtlənd ɪn də 'ɛrli 'twɪntiəθ 'sɛntjuri

kam ʌp fe hm 'kʌmri ən a ðat kaend ə 'plesiz əm dʒʌst 'fɔloɪn ðə 'hɛrɪŋ/

Millar:

/ae ae

ən ðer tʌŋs 'kɪnə 'karid ɔn ə wi bɪt/

Mary Blance:

/jas jas

du min də nemz ə də wɔts ðə 'waezmanz

ðers lɔts o 'dɪfərɪnt nemz ðat jɪl kʌm ə'krɔs kwar də fok ə'rɪdʒənali kam ʌp ən ðat/

Generally, Mary Blance keeps close to her native Shetland usage, notably in the use of plural *that* and the fairly regular employment of /d/ rather than the SSE /ð/, as well as merger or near-merger of GOAT, COT and CAUGHT. She does occasionally move quite far towards the SSE end of her personal linguistic continuum. This may have something to do with her radio journalism (although she regularly uses quite dense Shetland dialect in her broadcasts); again, the observer's paradox might be used to account for this. In her last sentence she distinctly realises /kwar/ for the expected /ʌar/. Although this merger is found with some Shetland varieties, locals would not associate it with her north mainland origin.

7.1.5 *Laureen Johnson, Voe, October 2005*

Laureen Johnson: You're likely seen de . . . de postcaird view . . . whi . . . as you kom in, ye ken, ye're turnin de corner an then it kinda just aw comes oot. Em . . . Every week – every week in summer – den dey're tourist

busses stappin an falk getting oot an angling fur de best shots or oni-
ething. Bit . . . eh . . . folk sometimes tinks at . . . eh . . . Voe looks a bit
Norwegian. Dey're speakin about like dat bit o Voe – de bonnie bit o Voe.
I dinna bide in de bonny bit. Dis is . . . dis is de . . . de kinda nandescript
bit o Voe. But de de bit doon at de sea apparently reminds falk o Norway.

aw: all; *bonnie:* beautiful, pretty; *bide:* stay, live

/jur 'ləikli sin də
də pɔst'kerd vju
ʌɪ
az ju kʌm ɪn
jɪ ken
jɪr 'tʌrnɪn ðə 'kɔrnər ən ðɛn ɪt 'kəində dʒʌst 'ɔpənz ut
əm
'ɪvri wik
'ɪvri de ɪn 'sʌmər
dɛn der 'turɪst 'bʌsɪs 'stapɪn ən fak 'gɛtɪn ut ən 'aŋglɪn fʌr də bɛst ʃɔts
    ər 'ɔniθɪŋ
bɪt ə
fɔk 'sʌmtaemz tɪŋks at ə
vo luks ə bɪt nɔr'widʒən
der 'spɪkɪn ə'but 'ləik dat bɪt ə vo
də 'bɔni bɪt ə vo
ae 'dɪnə bəid ɪn də 'bɔni bɪt
dɪs ɪz
dɪs ɪz
də
də 'kəində nan 'dɪskrɪpt bɪt o vo
bɪt də də bɪt dun ət də si ə 'perəntli rə 'maendz fak ə 'nɔrwe/

Laureen Johnson is a writer of some standing in both Shetland dialect
and English. It is fitting, therefore, that her speech should be among the
most Shetlandic recorded. Although she uses SSE /ð/ for Shetland /d/
on one occasion, a large part of the phonology – including /t/ where SSE
would have /θ/ – is consistently Shetland. There has been a near complete measure of GOAT, COT and TRAP, as witnessed in /fak/, 'folk',
recorded twice, and /nan'dɪskrɪpt/, 'nondescript'. That this merger is
only partial can be seen in the realisation of /fɔk/, 'folk' and /'ɔpənz/,
where only merger of GOAT and COT is apparent. TRY and BITE also
appear to have nearly merged (although perhaps not so thoroughly as
with the north isles). The /e/ pronunciation for the stressed vowel in

apparently is quite common throughout the Scots-speaking area.

There are also a number of typically Shetlandic structures in the text, including the *be*-perfective in *You're likely seen* and the *they + be* existential in *dey're tourist busses stappin*. One example of the Northern subject-noun concord rule is also present: *folk sometimes tinks.*

7.1.6 Iris Sandison and Bertie Jamieson, Walls and Sandness, western mainland of Shetland, October 2005

Iris Sandison: Although there's similarities atween Waas an Sandness, there great differences too in vowels.

Bertie Jamieson: Yeah. We *ken* things, bit you dinna.

Iris Sandison: We *ken* things

Bertie Jamieson: You *ken* things.

Iris Sandison: We *ken*. An whauras . . . em . . . we wöd spik aboot . . . em . . . A'll *tell* dee a story. Bertie, du wöd say:

Bertie Jamieson: A'll *tell* you a story.

Iris Sandison: *Tell.*

Bertie Jamieson: *Tell.* Harder.

Iris Sandison: An we wöd spik aboot a *gell* o win.

Bertie Jamieson: An we spik aboot a *gell.* That's why I thought you wöd say *well* instaid o *wall.*

Iris Sandison: Mhmhm Mhmhm. No, no. The *wall* is very much in Waas.

Bertie Jamieson: Intit funny, that. That's . . . that's. I wöd . . . uh . . . uh . . . expected du ti say *well.*

Iris Sandison: Bit then, if you start traivellin aroon Shetland, and you get a word like . . . wir . . . wir word fur cabbage in Waas wöd be *kell* [kail].

Bertie Jamieson: Yeah.

Iris Sandison: Is it *kell* or *kell* in Saaness?

Bertie Jamieson: No, it's *kell. Kell.*

Iris Sandison: Ha Ha!

Millar: An you use that fur cabbage?

Bertie Jamieson: Whit . . . whit dö you caa *lambs?*

Iris Sandison: *Lambs.*

Bertie Jamieson: *Lambs.*

Iris Sandison: Whit's du mean *lambs. Lambs.*

Bertie Jamieson: Young sheep.

Iris Sandison: Beee [imitates sheep]

Bertie Jamieson: Young sheep.

Iris Sandison: Jöst *lambs.*

Bertie Jamieson: My wife caad dem *lembs.*

Iris Sandison: *Lembs.*

Bertie Jamieson: *Lembs*.

Iris Sandison: O, yeah, wi de . . .

Bertie Jamieson: *Lembs*, dey spak aboot.

Iris Sandison: Dat's kind o like . . . eh . . . Coningsburgh.

Bertie Jamieson: Yeah well, dey're anidder story!

Iris Sandison: An dere's anidder story. Yeah.

atween: between; *ken*: know; *gell*: gale

Iris Sandison:
/al'ðo ðerz sɪməl'arətiz ə'twin waz ən 'sanəs der gret 'dɪfərənsiz tu ɪn
    vəuəls/

Bertie Jamieson:
/jɛ
wi kɛn [ɛ̌] θɪŋz
bɪt ju 'dɪnə/

Iris Sandison:
/wi kɛn [ɪ] θɪŋz/

Bertie Jamieson:
/ju kɛn [ɪ̞]/

Iris Sandison:
/wi kɛn [ɪ]
an 'ʍɔrəs əm wi wyd spɪk ə'but əm
al tɛl [ɪ̞] di ə 'stori 'bɛrti
du wyd se/

Bertie Jamieson:
/al tɛl [ɛ] ju ə 'stori/

Iris Sandison:
/tɛl [ɛ]/

Bertie Jamieson:
/tɛl [ɛ]
'hardər/

Iris Sandison:
/ən wi wyd spɪk ə'but ə gɛl [ɛ̌] o wɪn/

Bertie Jamieson:
/ən wi spɪk ə'but ə gɛl [ɛ]
ðats ʍae ae θɔt ju wyd se wɛl [ɛ] ən'sted o wal [a]/

Iris Sandison:
/əm'hm əm'hm
no no
ðə wal [aˑ] ɪz 'vɛri mʌtʃ ɪn waz/

Bertie Jamieson:

/ɪnt ɪt 'fʌni ðat

ðats ðats

ae wyd ə ə ək'spɛktəd du tə se wɛl [ɛ̝] /

Iris Sandison:

/bɪt dɛn

ɪf ju start 'trevələn ə'run 'ʃɛtlən

ən ju gɛt ə wʌrd laek

wɪr wɪr wʌrd fʌr 'kabɪdʒ ɪn waz wyd bi kɛl [ɛ] /

Bertie Jamieson:

/jɛ/

Iris Sandison:

/ɪz ɪt kɛl [ɛ] ɔr kɛl [ɛ̝] ɪn 'sanəs/

Bertie Jamieson:

/nɔ

ɪts kɛl [ɛ]

kɛl [ɛ] /

Iris Sandison:

/ha ha/

Millar:

/ən ju juz ðat fʌr 'kabɪdʒ/

Bertie Jamieson:

/ʍɪt

ʍɪt dy ju ka lamz [a]/

Iris Sandison:

/lamz [a]/

Bertie Jamieson:

/lamz [a]/

Iris Sandison:

/ʍɪts du min lamz [æ]

lamz [æ̝]/

Bertie Jamieson:

/jʌŋ ʃip/

Iris Sandison:

/bɛ/

Bertie Jamieson:

/jʌŋ ʃip/

Iris Sandison:

/dʒyst lamz [a]/

Bertie Jamieson:

/mae waef kad dem lɛmz [ɛ̝]/

Iris Sandison:

/lɛmz [ɛ]/

Bertie Jamieson:
/lemz [ɛ̞]/
Iris Sandison:
/ɔ jɛ wɪ də/
Bertie Jamieson:
/lemz [æ̞] de spak ə'but/
Iris Sandison:
/dats kaend o laek ə 'kʌnɪŋzbʌrə/
Bertie Jamieson:
/jɛ wɛl der ən'ɪdər 'stori/
Iris Sandison:
/ən ders ən'ɪdər 'stori
jɛ/

This is a fascinating discussion and exemplification of the level to which people's pronunciation can be localised in Shetland, and the extent to which locals perceive these differences. Walls and Sandness are little more than ten kilometres apart, but significant distinctions are to be found. In another part of the interview, Iris Sandison and Bertie Jamieson commented on the point that, until good roads were built in that part of Shetland in fairly recent times, the fact that Sandness is on the north side of the peninsula, while Walls is on the south, meant that the former had more to do with the northern settlements across St Magnus Bay than with Walls.

What is interesting, however, is that, with the exception of *lambs*, the reported shibboleths between the two settlements appear to be phonetic, rather than phonemic, with Iris Sandison generally having a pronunciation which is somewhat higher in the mouth than Bertie Jamieson's; there may on occasion also be length distinctions. With the assistance of Dom Watt, I have attempted a phonetic transcription of these vowels. Considerable variation in how and where /l/ is pronounced also appears to be used to distinguish between local pronunciations.

Beyond this, we find typical Shetland features, such as the merger or near merger of MATE-HAME and DRESS sets, and the TRY and BITE sets, as well as evidence for the /e/ pronunciation for the MEAT set in *instaid*. As with other Shetland informants, Mrs Sandison and Mr Jamieson code switch to quite an extent, using both /d/ and /ð/. The final exchange between the informants demonstrates a form of structural code-switching, with Iris Sandison employing a fairly standard *dere's* for *there is*, while Bertie Jamieson uses the specifically Shetland *dey're*. This is striking, because, in general, Bertie Jamieson uses the standard second-person pronoun rather than *du*, which might suggest that he is less comfortable than Iris Sandison, since it is her house where the recording is taking place.

7.1.7 Maria Leask, Lerwick. October 2005

Nooadays de dialects, dey're a lot mare blendit, an you can . . . you can jöst sometimes mak oot whaar folk are fae fae deir dialect. Bit whin I first startit workin A wis a shop assistant in wan o de local drapers doon in the Commercial Street, you could really tell den whaar folk were fae. Bit noo wi folk movin roond its . . . eh . . . its. An den de youngsters nooadays, dey jöst soon lik dey're fae de Scottish mainland. Dere's sich an int . . . sich an interest in de television. An mibbe a lot of the boys an lassies are both intae fuitbaa, so aa dey hir around dey is Scotland and de Scottish fuitbaa.

mare: more; *fae*: from; *soon*: sound; *fuitbaa*: football, soccer

/'nuədez də 'daeəlɛkts
der ə lɔt mer 'blɛndɪt
ən ju kan ju kan jyst 'sʌmtɪmz mak ut ʍar fok ər fe fe der daeəlɛkts
bɪt ʍɪn ae fɪrst 'startət 'wʌrkɪn a wɪz a ʃop ə'sɪstənt ɪn wan o ðə 'lokəl
   'drepərs dun
'ɪn də kə'mrʃəl strit
ju kyd 'rili tɛl dɛn ʍar fok wʌr fe
bɪt nu wi fok 'muvɪn rund ɪts ə ɪts
ən dɛn də 'jʌŋstərs 'nuədez
de dʒyst sun lɪk der fe də 'skɔtɪʃ 'menlənd
ders sɪtʃ ən ɪnt
sɪtʃ ən 'ɪntərɪst ɪn də tɛli'vɪʃɔn
ən 'mɪbi ə lɔt əv ðə bɔez ən 'lasiz ar boθ 'ɪnti 'fɪtba
so a de hɪr ə'rəund de ɪz 'skɔtlənd ən də 'skɔtɪʃ 'fɪtba/

Although Maria Leask is the youngest of our Shetland informants, being in her thirties, her use of the local dialect is impressively consistent, even though she is speaking to two outsiders. There are, for instance, only two occasions where she uses /ð/ instead of the local /d/. It might be significant that she is particularly committed to the recording and passing on of traditional folk dances, implying considerable commitment to the local community and its way of life. Unlike most other Shetland informants, she appears to keep MATE-HAME separate from DRESS. She does, however, have a lowered GOAT vowel in /boθ/. The use of the subject pronoun *dey* in object context is interesting, but may be a slip of the tongue, since it is not common in either colloquial English or in the local dialect.

7.2 Orkney

7.2.1 Allan Taylor, Kirkwall (born in the western mainland), August 2005

Ye see that Kirkwall is a great place. Aall the people who come fae the island o Westray, mibbe come ti live in Kirkwall, they still cling teegither, or the island o Sanday, or like fok fae Stenness. I meet them every day. So you have a great yarn aboot whitever pairish ye come tee yet, ye ken, the kinda older cheneration. That doesna affect the young folk so much, because they're all bussed in fur school, or drama clubs, or things like that. [I] mean, there's drama clubs. Bit in wur young days it wis mostly plooin matches wi horses or . . . or howin matches with . . . wi neeps, ye ken.

neeps: turnips, swedes

/ji si ðat 'kɪrkwəl ɪz ə gret ples
al ðə 'pipəl hu kʌm fe ðə 'əilənd o 'wɛstre 'mɪbi kʌm ti lɪv ɪn 'kɪrkwəl
ðe stɪl klɪŋ ti'gɪðər
ɔr ðə 'əilənd o 'sande
ɔr ləik fɔk fe stə'nɛs
ae mit ðɪm ɪ'vri de
so ju hɪv ə gret jarn ə'but ʌət'ɪvər 'perɪʃ ji kʌm ti jɛt
ji kɛn
ðə 'kəində 'oldər tʃɛnər'eʃən
ðat 'dʌznə ə'fɛkt ðə juŋ fɔk so mʌtʃ
'bikəz ðer al bʌsd ɪn fʌr ʃkul
ən 'dramə klʌbz ən θɪŋz lɪk ðat
min ðerz 'dramə klʌbz
bɪt ɪn wʌr jʌŋ de ɪt wɪz 'mostli 'pluən 'matʃiz wə 'hɔrsəz
ɔr ər 'həuən 'matʃiz wɪθ
wi nips
ji kɛn/

Allan Taylor's speech veers from quite SSE pronunciation (for instance, with /'mostli/) to highly local pronunciation (for instance, the rounded vowel in /juŋ/). A half-way house between the two poles is /al/ for *all*, containing the characteristic Northern and Insular Scots /a/ but without '/l/ dropping'. Towards the end of the excerpt, he also replaces Standard *with* with Scots *wi*. There appears to be at least partial merger between MATE-HAME and DRESS, particularly with /gret/ and /'perɪʃ/. There is also one example of the devoicing of /dʒ/ to /tʃ/: /tʃɛnər'eʃən/, which appears to be sporadic in Orkney, and possibly lexically triggered.

7.2.2 Neil Leask, St Ola, August 2005

We used ti hiv fok that came in an visited too in the evening. And actually – believe it or no – I think that's a thing that many youngsters noo hiv never experienced. It's so much a culture of jist the television on, or the fok come roon ti wattch a video, or they rarely mibbe sit and chat. An . . . an . . . very rare would fok be reminiscin aboot owlder times.

/wi just tə hɪv fɔk ðat kem ɪn ən 'vɪzətɪd tu ɪn ðə 'ivnɪŋ
and 'aktʃəli
bə'liv ɪt ər no
ae θɪŋk ðats ə θɪŋ ðət 'mɛni 'jʌŋstərʃ nu həv 'nɛvər ɛks'piriənst
ɪts so mʌtʃ ə 'kʌltjər əʌ dʒɪst ðə tɛlə'vɪʒən ɔn
ər ðə fɔk kʌm run tə watʃ ə 'vɪdio
ər ðe 'rerli 'mɪbi sɪt and tʃat
ən ən 'vɛri rer wud fɔk bi rɛmən'ɪsən ə'but 'əuldər təimz/

Although Neil Leask is only in his early thirties, and is obviously accommodating to some extent, it is surprising how much this remains a genuine representation of traditional local pronunciation, including the /ɔ/ pronunciation in *folk* and /a/ in *watch*. Perhaps most striking is the diphthongal pronunciation for *old*, an occasional feature of Orcadian speech. The use of the standard adverbial form /'rerli/ along with the non-standard /rer/ within moments of each other is also noteworthy. It may be that his rather 'old-fashioned' speech patterns stem from both his rural background and his employment in a museum which attempts to preserve material about the traditional lifestyles of Orkney.

7.3 Caithness

7.3.1 Murray Banks, Cathy Oag and Jenny Szyfelbain, Wick, February 2006

Jenny Szyfelbain: It wis a cosmopolitan port, cause they're wis a lot came back an fore in it. Ti fit we've got now, which is a port full of nothingness.
Millar: Ay. A wis quite saddened bi that. A wis oot . . .

Jenny Szyfelbain It iz ... aw ... It ... it ... it breaks ma hert. [If] ma
father came back an seen that ... e ... e ... e. e jist wid be devastated.

Murray Banks: He'd no want ti come back, Jenny.

Jenny Szyfelbain: Eh?

Murray Banks: He widna want til come back.

Jenny Szyfelbain: No, no, no.

Murray Banks: Mind they beelt a new fish mart. Dod knows how many
thousands ...

Jenny Szyfelbain: Wi EEC funding of course.

Murray Banks: Wi EEC funding.

Jenny Szyfelbain: An we're no a designated port. A don't think there wis
ever a fish landed intil this there.

Murray Banks: No, it's up fur sale or rent.

Millar: Ay, wi nae buyers.

Cathy Oag: The blessin o ay fleet at ay Gallow-way.

Murray Banks: O Jeens [Jings?]. Yun's hypocrisy.

Cathy Oag: That's whit A wis in.

Jenny Szyfelbain: Well, as lieve it [believe it?]. They rehashed dat two
year ago. An Raymond hid sayed summat at ay toime: you have no fleet
til bless.

Jenny Szyfelbain:
/ɪt wəz ə kɔzmoˈpɔlɪtən port
kəz ðer wəz ə lɔt kem bak ən for ɪn ɪt
ti fʌt wiv gɔt nəu
ʍɪtʃ ɪz ə port ful ə ˈnɔθɪŋnəs/

Millar:
/ae
a wɪz kwəit ˈsadənd bə ðat
a wɪz ut/

Jenny Szyfelbain
/ɪt ɪz
ɔ
ɪt ɪt ɪt breks ma hərt
ma ˈfaðər kem bak ən sin ðat
i i i i dʒɪst wɪd bi dɛvəsˈtetəd/

Murray Banks:
/hɪd no want ti kʌm bak ˈdʒɛni/

Jenny Szyfelbain:
/e/

Murray Banks:
/hi wɪdnə want tɪl kʌm bak/

Jenny Szyfelbain:

/no no no/
Murray Banks:
/məind ðe bilt ə nju fiʃ mart
dɔd nos həu mɛni 'θəuzəndz/
Jenny Szyfelbain:
/wi i i si 'fʌndɪŋ əv kɔrʃ/
Murray Banks:
/wi i i si 'fʌndɪŋ/
Jenny Szyfelbain:
/ən wir no ə 'dɛzɪgnetət port
a dont θɪŋk ðer wəz 'ɪvər ə fiʃ 'landəd 'ɪntɪl ðɪs ðer/
Murray Banks:
/no ɪts ʌp fʌr sel ər rɛnt/
Millar:
/ae wi ne 'baeərs/
Cathy Oag:
/ðə 'blɛsɪn o e flit at e 'galowe/
Murray Banks:
/o 'dʒiənz jʌnz hɪp'ɔkrəsi/
Cathy Oag:
/ðats ʍɪt a wɪz ɪn/
Jenny Szyfelbain:
/wɛl əz'liv ɪt
ðe 'rihaʃd dat tu jir ə'go
an 'remənd hɪd sed 'sʌmət at e tɔim
ju hav no flit tɪl blɛs/

Although occasional SSE pronunciations are present in this excerpt, it is remarkable how many Caithness usages are found, including a 'rolled' /r/, e/ for *the*, an 'open' diphthong /ɔi/ for what is /əi/ in most Scots dialects (although it should be noted that Murray Banks uses /əi/). There are a number of examples of Caithness final /d/ where other Scots dialects (and often SSE) would have /t/, such as /dɛvəs'tetəd/. There is one occasion, /'rihaʃd dat/, where the /d/ (rather than /t/) at the end of the first word seems to have encouraged a stop rather than fricative pronunciation in the second word. But there is at least one occasion (from the same speaker), /'dɛzɪgnetət/, where /t/ appears to be realised. It should be noted, however, that the /t/ pronunciations are heavily glottalised (suggesting, perhaps, a 'modern' colloquial English transfer); the final /t/ may have been influenced by the following /p/ in /port/. There also seems to be merger or near-merger between MATE-HAME and DRESS. On at least one occasion, /bilt/ for *built*, KIT words are pronounced as MEET. In one example, /hɔrt/, Scots *hert*, 'heart', we have coalescence of PERCH and at least HURT. Although /f/ for /ʍ/ is realised on one occasion, SSE /ʍ/ is also present.

Perhaps the most striking feature of this recording is the speed with which the informants speak. This is something which Caithness people comment about themselves. Certainly it makes their speech unique in northern Scotland.

7.4 Black Isle

7.4.1 Jean Newell, Cromarty, October 2005

The fishing community were completely different from the rest of us, in that they had their own language which they kept for themselves, and och . . . 'Art thee sick en?' [Are you sick, then?]; 'Ar thee gaein?' [Where are you going?]; 'At a pretty at dee have on' [What a pretty hat you have on]; 'A telt ee' [I told you]. Now, they kept that language really for themselves among them the . . . and when they came to school it was a different thing . . . conformed.

/ðə ˈfɪʃɪŋ kəmˈjunɪti wɛr kəmˈplitli ˈdɪfərənt frɔm ðə rɛst əv ʌz
ɪn ðat ðe had ðɪr on ˈlaŋgwɪdʒ ʍɪtʃ ðe kɛpt fɔr ðəmˈsɪlvz
and ʌx
art ði sik ɛn
ar ði ˈgeən
at ə ˈprɪti at ði hav ɔn
a tɛlt ti
nəu ðə kɛpt ðat ˈlaŋgwɪdʒ ˈrili fər ðəmˈsɪlvz əˈmʌŋ ðɪm ðə
and ʍɛn ðe kem tə skul ɪt wəz ə ˈdɪfərənt θɪŋ
kənˈfɔrmd/

Mrs Jean Newell is the oldest resident of Cromarty. Her own pronunciation could be described as educated Highland English, although her consistent pronunciation of *themselves*, /ðəmˈsɪlvz/, is intriguing. She also uses among the few back /u/ heard on mainland Scotland during the fieldwork carried out for this book. Her memory of the fisher language of her youth is fascinating, including examples of /h/ and /ʍ/ dropping, as well as the preservation of a specifically second-person singular pronoun. Obviously a gifted mimic, her examples include a considerable number of assimilation features, not least in the apparent assimilation of initial /ð/ to final /t/ in /a tɛlt ti/.

7.5 Mid-Northern B

7.5.1 Mhairi Duncan, Aberdeen (native of Elgin), February 2006

We stayed in a . . . a little house jist off one o the . . . the main streets, and we had everythin around about us, ye know: had a wee Spar; had a wee . . . a sweetie shop as well, which, ye know, for a wee kid growin up in Elgin, that's . . . that's whit you're lookin for. We were just five minutes away from the local school an en about ten minutes away from the academy when A . . . when A went up there. So A had everythin round about me. We had a, like a wood just up the back of our house. It wis good fur the dog. An so we could go up there an go cycling in the woods. So A think it wis great.

/wi sted ɪn ə ə 'lɪtəl həus dʒɪst ɔf wʌn o ðə ðə men strits
ənd wi had 'ɪvriθɪn ə'rəund ə'bəut ʌz
jə no
had ə wi spar
had ə wi
ə 'switi ʃɔp əz wɛl
ʌɪtʃ
jə no
fər ə wi kɪd 'groɪn ʌp ɪn 'ɛlgɪn
ðats
ðats ʌɪt jur 'lukɪn fɔr
wi wər dʒɪst faev 'mɪnɪts ə'we frəm ðə 'lokəl skul ən ɛn ə'bəut tɛn 'mɪnɪts ə'we frəm ðə ə'kadəmi ʌɪn a
ʌɪn a wɛnt ʌp ðer
so a had 'ɪvriθɪn rəund ə'bəut mi
wi had a
ləik ə wud dʒʌst ʌp ðə bak əv əur həus
ɪt wəz gud fər ðə dɔg
ən so wi kud go ʌp ðer
ən go 'səiklɪŋ ɪn ðə wudz
so a θɪŋk ɪt wəz gret/

It is informative to compare Mhairi Duncan's speech with her near contemporary, Beverley Buchanan (both women are in their early to mid-twenties) (see 7.6.2). Almost all of Mhairi Duncan's speech is Scottish Standard English, with a few, probably largely unconscious, non-standard features, such as the use of /a/ for Standard *I*, or /n/ instead of Standard /ŋ/. Other Scots features she uses are intriguing, such as the use of /ʌɪn/, the usual Central Belt equivalent to *when*, rather than the local /fɪn/. This orientation towards more mainstream Scots varieties may also be seen in her use of a very front allophone of /u/, which marks her speech off from that found in older people's speech in her native region. It may be that in this excerpt we find evidence for what most people's speech in the North-East will sound like in a few generations. This is particularly striking, since she is obviously very well-disposed towards her home town.

7.6 Mid-Northern A

7.6.1 Robert Bruce, Peterhead, November 2005

Jock'll mibbe come doon an he'll say: 'Hiv you got sik-an-sich'. An he'll hae it mibbe fur a fortnight, ken, an he'll: 'Here ye go an this is it, bit A'll gie you something fur at now'. It . . . A mean . . . it wis a fantastic wey ti work, cause there wis one time he come inti e garage – he's a character – an . . . eh . . . he says, 'Hiv you got a petrol can' – now this is jist how they think. I says, 'Ay, A think A hiv, Jock. Now, now: here ye go.' 'Ay, A'll suppose A'll hae ti waalk doon ti Crookie's garage fur petrol.' Pause. A sayed, 'Jump in e car, Jock, an . . . eh . . . okay, A'll tak ye doon' – hees car wis jist tucked awaa here somewhere. So, 'Jist you follae behind me, now, in case I . . . me car disna make it.' 'Ay, okay, Jock'.

So A wis deein e central heatin – an is is a lot o years ago – an A haaled oot e fireplace, an it wis jist a pile o rubble, an A jist left it at that. So, fin A follaed him hame, he says: 'See at rubble at's lyin outside yer . . . yer hoose? Fit ye gaanie dee wi it?' 'Nae idea', A says, 'A never really thocht aboot it cause A'm nae finished', A said, 'Well A'll hae ti get rid o it; fitever'. 'Well, Michael'll be doon e night an he'll tidy it up fur you' – is is wi his boy – 'an at's us quits, bud.'

sik: such

/dʒɔkl 'mɪbi kʌm dun an hil se
əv ju gɔt 'sɪkənsɪtʃ
ən hil he ɪt 'mɪbi fər ə fɔrt'nəit
kɛn
ən il
hir ji go ən ðɪs ɪz ɪt
bɪt al gi ju 'sʌmθɪŋ fər at nəu
ɪt
a min
ɪt wəz ə fən'tastɪk wae tə wʌrk

kəz ðer wɪz wʌn təim hi kʌm 'ɪntə ə 'garɪdʒ
iz ə 'karəktər
ən e
i sez
əv ju gɔt ə 'pɛtrəl kan
nəu ɪs ɪz jɪst həu ðe θɪŋk
a sɛz
ae a θɪŋk a hɪv dʒɔk
nəu nəu hir ji go
ae al sə'poz al he tə wak dun tə 'krukiz 'garɪdʒ fər 'pɛtrəl
pɔz
a sed
dʒʌmp ɪn ə kar dʒok
ən e
o ke al tak ji dun
iz kar wəz dʒɪst tʌkt ə'wa hir 'sʌmʌər
so
dʒɪst ju 'fɔli bə'həind mi nəu
ɪn kes əi
mi kar 'dɪznə mek ɪt
ae o ke dʒɔk
so a wɪz 'diən ə 'sɛntrəl 'hitən
ən ɪs ɪz ə lɔt ə jirs ə'go
ən a hald ut ə 'fəirples
ən ɪt wəz dʒɪst ə pəil ə 'rʌbəl
ən a dʒɪst lɛft ɪt ət ðat
so fɪn a 'fɔlid əm hem
i sez
si at 'rʌbəl əts 'laeɪn 'utsəid jər jər hus
fɪt ji 'gani di wi ət
nə ae'diə
a sez
a 'nɪvər 'rili θɔxt ə'but ɪt kəz am ne 'fɪnɪʃt
a sɛd
wəl al he tə gɛt rɪd i ɪt
fət'ɪvər
so a sez
o ae
wəl 'məikəl əl bi dun ə nəit
ən hil 'təidi ɪt ʌp fɔr ju
ɪs ɪz wi ɪz bɔe
ən ats ʌz kwɪts bʌd/

Although there are a number of SSE features in Robert Bruce's speech, it is striking how North-East his language is. This includes the characteristic /f/ pronunciation for <wh>, the elision of /ð/ with pronouns, the pronunciation of BUIT words with /i/ in /di/, 'do', the merger or near-merger of /e/ and /ɛ/ and the TRY vowel in /wae/. The elision of /h/ in pronouns in unstressed environments is certainly in line with many Scots dialects, although it may be more prevalent in fishing communities in Buchan than elsewhere. He also uses the characteristic (but now disappearing) /x/ in *thocht*, 'thought'. Noteworthy also is the 're-stressed' pronoun /hiz/.

7.6.2 Beverley Buchanan, Boddam, by Peterhead, November 2005

Tryin ti think o mare fin . . . fit used ti get picked up ti me fin A bed doon in Grangemouth, because they used ti pick up words fae me aa the time, an ask fit at meant, cause A worked in a hairdressers doon ere – A wiz a hairdresser ti trade – an they were ayeways askin me fit . . . fit ye sayin, ken. Well, it wis 'Whit are ye sayin?' A lot o them didna understaan fur wiks. A bed in Glesga an aa fur a while. An the quine A bed wi, she says, 'Why d'ye ask?', she says, 'See fin ye say "O, at's right fine, is it?"', she says, 'Are ye expectin me ti answer, or is it just a statement?' A wis like, 'A dinna ken: A've nae thought about it'.

fin: when; *fit:* what; *bed:* lived, stayed; *ayeways:* always; *quine:* young woman, girl

/ˈtraeən tə θɪŋk o mer fɪn
fɪt just te gɛt pɪkt ʌp tə mə fɪn a bɛd dun ɪn ˈgrɛndʒməuθ
bəˈkɔz ðe just tə pɪk ʌp wʌrdz fe mə a ðə təim
ən ask fɪt at mɛnt
kəz a wʌrkt ɪn ə ˈherdrɛsərz dun er
a wɪz ə ˈherdrɛsər tə tred
ən ðe wər ˈəiwez ˈaskən mə fɪt
fɪt ji ˈseən
kɛn
wɛl ɪt wɪz ʌɪt ər ji ˈseən
a lɔt o ðəm ˈdɪdnə ʌndərˈstan fər wɪks
a bɛd ɪn ˈglezgə ən a fər ə ʌɪl
ɛn ðə kwəin a bɛd wi
ʃi sɛz
ʌae dji ask
ʃi sɛz

si fɪn jə se
o ats rəit fəin ɪz ɪt
ʃə səz
ar jə ək'spɛktən mi tə 'ʌnsər
ɔr ɪz ɪt dʒʌst ə 'stetmənt
a wɪz ləik
a 'dɪnə kɛn
av ne θɔt ə'but ɪt/

There are a number of SSE features in Beverley Buchanan's speech. These are much outweighed, however, by the number of local features realised, such as /f/ for <wh>, the elision of /ð/ with pronouns and the use of local /ne/, the equivalent of SSE *not*. Particularly striking is her pronunciation of *answer* as /'ʌnsər/. The stories she tells of her time in the Central Belt demonstrates both the diversity of speech patterns in Scotland and her awareness of her own usage, not just phonologically, but also structurally. When we compare her speech to that of her father, Robert Bruce, it is apparent that Scots has continued as a living medium in her family.

7.7 South Northern

7.7.1 Kevin Durward, Hillside, June 2005

It wis Hi. . . the village o Hillside I wis brought up. A steyed there . . . A've steyed there near aa ma life. A've still goat a strong connection wi it yit . . . e . . . A think aa ma young days A wis mainly jist doon at the ferm aa the time. A jist grew up on the ferm jist. Aahin . . . aahin revolved aroon the ferm. An A think that wis how A wis so thick at schail, because aahin jist revolved aroon the ferm. Ye aye . . . A jist wantit tae come hame at night . . . Ken, fae first thing in the morning ye jist wanted tae come hame at night an say, 'ferm'. That's aa at wis in ma heid. And, eh . . . I . . . I . . . hud a lot o opportunities. I think . . . eh . . . for my experience I think I learned mare outside the schail than Ah actually did inside the schail.

steyed: stayed; *ferm*: farm; *jist*: just; *aahin*: everything; *schail*: school; *hame*: home; *heid*: head

/ɪt wɪz hɪ
ðə 'vɪlədʒ o 'hɪlsəid əi wɪz brɔt ʌp
a stəid ðer
av stəid ðer nir a ma ləif

av stɪl gɔt a strɔŋ kən'ɛkʃən we ɪt jɪt
ɛ
a θɪŋk a ma jʌŋ dez a wɪz 'menli dʒɪst dun ət ðə fɛrm a ðə təim
a dʒɪst gru ʌp ɔn ðə fɛrm dʒɪst
a'hɪn
a'hɪn rə'vɔlvd ə'run ðə fɛrm
ən a θɪŋk ðat wɪz həu a wɪz so θɪk ət skel
bɪ'kɔz a hɪn dʒɪst rə'vɔlvd ə'run ðə fɛrm
ji əi
a dʒɪst 'wɔntɪt ti kʌm hem ət nəit
kɛn
fe fɪrst θɪŋ ɪn ðə mɔrnɪŋ ji dʒɪst 'wɔntɪt ti kʌm hem ət nəit ən se
kɛn
fɛrm
ðats a ət wɪz ɪn ma hid
ənd ɛ
ae ae hʌd ə lɔt o ɔpər'tjunɪtis
ae θɪŋk
ɛ
fɔr mae ɛks'pirɪəns ae θɪŋk ae lɛrnd mer ut'səid ðə skel ðan a 'akʃuli dɪd
   ɪn'səid ðə skel/

As can be seen from this excerpt, Kevin Durward possesses considerable abilities in story-telling, using repetition as a rhetorical effect. Despite being in his thirties, his speech is representative of traditional dialect of the South Northern area; specifically, northern Angus. In phonological terms, his speech demonstrates partial GOAT-COT merger, as well as an /e/ reflex for BUIT. Three features of his speech which demonstrate some influence from the Central Belt, however, are the development of /θ/ to /h/ in /a'hɪn/, *aathin*, 'everything', glottalisation, particularly prominent in the /t/ in /ut'səid/, and the lack of 'strength' in the pronunciation of /r/, particularly noticeable with *ferm*. Although he uses the SSE /nəit/ and /brɔt/ in this excerpt, he regularly uses /x/ in its Scots positions elsewhere in the interview. Other SSE features include /mɔrnɪŋ/ and the half-Scots, half-SSE /'wɔntɪt/.

Index